WHEN
God
Speaks

RECEIVING AND WALKING IN
SUPERNATURAL REVELATION

Chuck D. Pierce
and
Rebecca Wagner Sytsema

WAGNER
PUBLICATIONS

When God Speaks
Copyright © 2003
by Chuck D. Pierce and Rebecca Wagner Sytsema
ISBN 1-58502-026-5
Library of Congress Control Number: 2002117005

Published by
Wagner Publications
11005 N. Highway 83
Colorado Springs, CO 80921
www.wagnerpublications.org

Cover design by
Imagestudios
100 East St. Suite 105, Colorado Springs, CO 80903
719-578-0351

Edited by C. Lil Walker

Interior design by Rebecca Sytsema

Rights for publishing this book in other languages are contracted by Gospel Literature International (GLINT). GLINT also provides technical help for the adaptation, translation, and publishing of Bible study resources and books in scores of languages worldwide. For further information, contact GLINT, P.O. Box 4060, Ontario, CA 91761-1003, USA. You may also send e-mail to glintint@aol.com, or visit their web site at www.glint.org.

1 2 3 4 5 6 7 8 9   09 08 07 06 05 04 03

Contents

Hearing the voice of God is not as difficult as some might think. I have found that many of God's people are hearing Him, but have not perceived that it is His voice. To perceive means to take hold of, feel, comprehend, grasp mentally, recognize, observe, or become aware of something by discerning. We must learn to perceive God's voice, which will help us understand His will for our lives. Acting upon what we have discerned as His voice until it becomes a reality is the key to a successful Christian life.

To commune with a holy God—you talking to Him and He to you—is the highest privilege we have on earth. My own life has become one of hearing the Lord's voice, not just for myself but for others as well. My greatest desire is for each person to hear God's voice, embrace His word, and fulfill the destiny God has for them.

I pray that this book will give you the principles of hearing God through prophecy and revelation, show you how to test and evaluate the prophetic word, and help you know what to do with that which God has spoken to you. As you read this book may you recognize the Voice that gives you life and life abundantly!

Chuck D. Pierce
Denton, Texas

CHAPTER ONE

Hear Him!

"Then God said, 'Let Us make man in Our image, according to Our likeness; let them have dominion over the fish of the sea, over the birds of the air, and over the cattle, over all the earth and over every creeping thing that creeps on the earth.' So God created man in His own image; in the image of God He created him; male and female He created them. Then God blessed them, and God said to them, 'Be fruitful and multiply; fill the earth and subdue it; have dominion over the fish of the sea, over the birds of the air, and over every living thing that moves on the earth.'"
(Genesis 1:26-28)

From the beginning of creation, humanity was created to commune with God. Because God's triune character of body, soul, and spirit was placed within us, we were given a different value from the rest of creation. We were made as spiritual beings. Our human spirit allows us to exercise intelligence, perception, determination, moral choices, and enables us to exceed above and have dominion over any other creature in the earth realm. This intrinsic worth drives us to know our Creator as well as to know the hope of our calling and why we exist.

Because we are set apart in this way, we also carry an accountability and responsibility that the rest of creation does not have. We are expected to be faithful stewards of the talents and abilities that God has given us. The only way we can do this is to seek Him, commune with Him, and gain the revelation that will enable us to prosper. When we obey this revelation from Him, we please Him.

We Were Created to Commune with Him Daily

The spirit is the highest function of our being. It is through our spirit that we commune with the spiritual world. When we open our human spirit and allow the Holy Spirit to come and reside within us, we come into a holy union with our Creator. It is through our human spirits that the Holy Spirit gives us the revelation necessary to accomplish His will on the earth. Because this is an ongoing process, we should expect God to commune with us daily as we seek Him. He longs for us to draw near to Him so we can know His heart and greatest desire for our life.

To seek means to diligently look for and search earnestly until the object of desire is located and found. Psalm 27:4-8 says, "One thing I have desired of the LORD, That will I seek: That I may dwell in the house of the LORD All the days of my life, To behold the beauty of the LORD, And to inquire in His temple. For in the time of trouble He shall hide me in His pavilion; In the secret place of His tabernacle He shall hide me; He shall set me high upon a rock. And now my head shall be lifted up above my enemies all around me; Therefore I will offer sacrifices of joy in His tabernacle; I will sing, yes, I will sing praises to the LORD. Hear, O LORD, when I cry with my voice! Have mercy also upon me, and answer me. When You said, 'Seek My face,' My heart said to You, ''Your face, LORD, I will seek.'''

David was known as a man with a heart after God because he was willing to seek God until he received the Lord's mind and strategy for that hour. That is also why Jesus said, "But seek first the kingdom of God and His righteousness, and all these things shall be added to you" (Matt. 6:33).

Moses gives us a beautiful example of and reason why we should be seeking God on a daily basis. In Exodus 29, we find that Moses is receiving revelation on the daily offerings two times each day. Here we see that the day is opened and closed with the gift of worship to and communion with God. Verse 42 says, "This shall be a continual burnt offering throughout your generations at the door of the tabernacle of meeting before the LORD, *where I will meet you to speak with you*" (emphasis added).

What a wonderful principle for us! If we will come before God on a daily basis, He will meet us, join with us, and speak to us. He will set us apart for service. We will begin to sense His presence. We will have assurance that He is with us. He will take a stand against our enemies. "And they shall know that I am the Lord their God who brought them out..." (verse 46). We will know that He is the God who will keep us safe, deliver us from evil, and lead us into all the promises and destiny He has for our lives.

Knowing God Speaks

I was eight years old when I first became aware that God had a voice and actually spoke to people. My godly grandmother would take me to a little Baptist church in East Texas where we lived. In that church was a lady named Mrs. Grimes who would do a very peculiar thing. Right in the middle of the preacher's message, Mrs. Grimes would stand up and wave her hands. Being a Baptist church, this was very unusual behavior. Yet the preacher would stop his message and ask her what was happening. Mrs. Grimes would say, "The Lord is speaking to me!" Then the pastor would say, "Tell us what He's saying." And Mrs. Grimes would begin to tell us what she was hearing from the Spirit of God and how it affected the church.

It totally fascinated me that God could really speak to people today. When the preacher talked about God, it seemed boring and dry. But when Mrs. Grimes would speak up, it was filled with life and vibrancy. I would look up at my grandmother and say, "If God can speak to that woman, I want Him to speak to me." My grandmother would look down at a typically wild eight-year-old boy and say, "You will have to learn to be quiet and sit still for God to ever say anything to you!"

My Day of Salvation

From that point on there was no question in my mind that God had a voice. I had heard it through Mrs. Grimes, and I heard it in the Bible stories taught in Sunday School. Still, I had never heard Him speak directly to me—until I was eleven years old. One Sunday during a service, the Spirit of the Lord came to me and clearly said, "This is your day." It was as if I followed His Spirit up to the altar and surrendered my life to Him as best as an eleven-year-old can.

As I studied the Bible later on, it became clear to me that God has a day of salvation for each one of us (see 2 Cor. 6:2). We all come into our day of salvation by hearing God's voice speak into our spirit, which up to that point is dead in trespasses. As we respond to His voice and allow Him to illuminate truth in our darkened spirit, we come into our day of salvation. In fact, none of us has been saved without the voice of God prompting us.

We may not have heard an audible voice, but because only God can illuminate the truth of salvation, everyone who has had a salvation experience and knows Jesus as their Lord and Savior has heard God's voice, whether or not they understood it at the time! It is this same voice that quickens the Word of God to us. Therefore, every time we glean truth from Scripture, we are hearing God at some level.

"I Will Restore"

Even though I had been saved, I had a difficult, often traumatic, and abusive childhood. Our family had suffered great loss and anguish. Much of our family fell apart through my teen years as a result of the enemy's inroads into my father's life. He then died under tragic circumstances when I was 16. By the time I was 18 my body had begun to suffer from the working, going to college, and having a fairly ardent nightlife.

Eventually I wound up in the hospital suffering from exhaustion and double pneumonia. It was while I was in the hospital that the Lord clearly spoke to me in an audible voice and said, "I will restore all that you have lost." With those words He penetrated every part of my being. Though I had suspected it before, I then *knew* that God had a plan not only to go back and heal the wounds of my past, but to restore my future.

I had never seen the concept of restoration in the Bible, but as I read more deeply, I learned that God's voice had the power to restore (see Joel 2:25). My whole life changed from that instant. God has healed, delivered, and restored me in miraculous ways.[1] God's voice has great power to bring us out of the ruins of our past and set us on the course He has ordained for our lives, as I learned that day many years ago.

Your Testimony

As you are reading, this may be a good place for you to stop and think about how the voice of God has manifested in your life. How were you saved? How has God supernaturally affected your life and your circumstances? You might want to write out your testimony. The reason for that is that there is great power in the word of our testimony because it builds faith as nothing else can.

Our testimony is an important function of the human spirit. Think of the Ark of God's covenant. Within the ark were several items. One of the items was the testament that God gave to Moses. When we commune with God through the Word, we store His precepts and principles down deep in our hearts, where we have established covenant with God. When we obey these precepts and principles, and experience God's faithfulness, we develop a testimony that has great power against our enemy. Once we have an established testimony, we can refute the lies of the devil by saying, "God has spoken this to me. Because I have seen His hand move in the past, I know He will do the same now, for nothing is impossible for Him!"

Revelation 12:10 says, "Then I heard a loud voice saying in heaven, 'Now salvation, and strength, and the kingdom of our God, and the power of His Christ have come, for the accuser of our brethren, who accused them before our God day and night, has been cast down.' And they overcame him by the blood of the Lamb and by the word of their testimony." The enemy cannot withstand the voice of God coupled with the power of our testimony.

God's Voice Is Creative

In the account of creation in Genesis, we see that the creative instrument God used again and again was His voice. God *spoke* into chaos and light came into being. He *spoke* again and light divided from darkness, creating day and night. The power of His voice created the heavens and earth, and the abundance of creatures filled the earth and seas.

God's voice is so powerful that it can divide substance. From the power of His voice, substance could be made into a different form.

God made the ground from His creative voice and from that ground He formed human beings. Our very being is, therefore, a product of His creative voice.

Jesus Speaks

Jesus was God as man come to earth to redeem the human race and to present the full character of God to us. Part of that character was the power of His voice. When Jesus spoke, things would happen. His public ministry began in John 2 when He and His mother attended a wedding. As the wedding feast ran short of wine, Jesus' mother told the servants, "Whatever He says to you, do it" (Jn. 2:5). It was Jesus' creative voice (the creative voice of God through Jesus as God and man) that changed the water into wine.

Whenever Jesus spoke, He carried great authority. When He raised Lazarus from the dead, Jesus *spoke* to the grave and to the shroud of death surrounding Lazarus, and commanded them to loose Lazarus and let him go. Upon His command, life processes once again began to flow through Lazarus. So powerful was His voice, that even death and decay were overcome and destroyed.

The Holy Spirit Speaks To and Through

The Holy Spirit was released to operate in greater measure in the transitional chapter of John 20. Jesus had already been crucified, died, and raised from the dead, but had not yet ascended to heaven. Jesus knew that He had to equip His disciples with power to accomplish their role on earth because He was now leaving to be with the Father. In John 20:22 we read that "He breathed on them, and said to them, 'Receive the Holy Spirit.'"

As the Holy Spirit was released to them, He began to speak *to* them and *through* them on an ongoing basis. The Holy Spirit spoke many times to them, including when He instructed Peter to go to the house of Cornelius. But prophecy was birthed in a whole new way as the Holy Spirit began to speak *through* them on a consistent basis. In Acts, the account of Stephen records, "and they were not able to resist the wisdom and the Spirit by which he spoke" (Acts 6:10). Here the Holy Spirit spoke *through* Stephen.

The Word Speaks

In addition to each member of the Trinity having a voice, God has also supplied us with His written word to speak into our lives. God told Joshua, "Only be strong, and very courageous, that you may observe to do according to all the law which Moses My servant commanded you. Do not turn from it to the right or to the left, that you may prosper wherever you go. This Book of the Law shall not depart from your mouth, but you shall mediate in it day and night that you may observe to do all that is written in it. For then you will make your way prosperous, and then you will have good success" (Joshua 1:7-8).

There is absolutely no Scripture in the Bible which even suggests that God stopped speaking when the last word of the Bible was written.

In the New Testament we find in John 1:14, "And the Word became flesh and dwelt among us, and we beheld His glory, the glory as of the only begotten of the Father, full of grace and truth." This Scripture describes the unique, loving relationship of the Son with the Father, and how we understand that relationship through the Word. By meditating on the Word, we reflect, ponder, contemplate, and repeat God's will for our life. We remove all distraction so it's just us and God interacting. His Word becomes a light to our path. As we order our prayers and communion, His Word orders our feet. His truths and principles guide us. By knowing the Word of God, we know Him and can recognize His voice and how He operates in the earth. The Word is the blueprint of heaven and the blueprint of life. "Today, if you will hear His voice, do not harden your hearts as in the rebellion" (Heb. 3:15).

God's Voice in Our Lives

Every member of the Trinity operates powerfully through speaking. God's voice commands great authority and continues to be creative today, even in our life situations. Whenever our lives are filled with chaos, as the heavens and earth once were, God's voice can come into our situation and bring order, dividing the light from the darkness.

Furthermore, God speaks to us more often than we may be aware. Consider the fact that throughout the Bible, in both the Old and New Testaments, God spoke to His people frequently. He spoke to the kings, the judges, the prophets, the shepherds, and the disciples. He spoke to old and young alike. He spoke to those in powerful positions, and to those with no social status. He spoke to the righteous and the sinner. From Genesis to Revelation, God was speaking to all kinds of people.

There is absolutely no Scripture in the Bible which even suggests that God stopped speaking when the last word of the Bible was written. Throughout the ages, God has continued to speak to His people. If you have accepted Christ as your Savior and Lord, that includes you! He speaks direction, comfort, insight, correction, exhortation, promises, and the like to His people today. "Anyone who is willing to hear should listen to the Spirit and understand what the Spirit is saying…" (Revelation 2:7, NLT).

Today, because we have been redeemed by the blood of Jesus, the Holy Spirit is locking us into the Father's heart for us. But here again, the Holy Spirit is not only speaking *to* us, but *through* us. When God formed us with His creative voice, He made us in His image, according to His likeness, and gave us dominion over all the earth (see Gen. 1:26). Because we are created in His image, and have been redeemed by Christ, therefore we have the ability, through the power of the Holy Spirit, *to be the voice of God on the earth.* The Holy Spirit is speaking through us to one another, and to a lost and dying world. That is what it means to be an ambassador for Christ, and that is what prophecy is all about.

Notes

[1]   A more complete account of this story is written in Chuck D. Pierce and Rebecca Wagner Sytsema, *Possessing Your Inheritance*, (Renew Books, 1999).

CHAPTER TWO

Speaking God's Words:
Prophecy in
Today's World

*"And it shall come to pass in the last days, says God, that I will
pour out of My Spirit on all flesh; your sons and your daughters
shall prophesy, your young men shall see visions, your old men
shall dream dreams"* (Acts 2:17).

Is Prophecy For Today?

Most Christians in the United States today grew up in churches
that did not embrace the idea of God speaking to us today. We
were taught "cessationism," which means that the power gifts of healing, tongues, interpretation of tongues, miracles, and the like all ceased
to function sometime in the first century. One of the gifts that suppos-
edly stopped functioning was prophecy. What that basically means is
that God said all He had to say by 95 A.D., and He has been silent ever
since.

Those who hold to this line of thinking believe that prophecy passed away when the Scriptures were completed. They base their belief on 1 Corinthians 13:8-9 which says that prophecy, tongues, and knowledge will pass away. However, Paul encourages us in the following chapter to desire prophecy (1 Cor. 14:1). He did not say that these gifts would be replaced by any others, nor that they would pass away before the second coming of Christ.

In fact, in Ephesians 4 Paul writes, "And He Himself gave some to be apostles, some prophets, some evangelists, and some pastors and teachers, for the equipping of the saints for the work of ministry, for the edifying of the body of Christ, *till we all come to the unity of the faith and of the knowledge of the Son of God, to a perfect man, to the measure of the stature of the fullness of Christ*" (Eph. 4:11-13, italics added).

In this passage we see that these gifts have been given *until* we come to unity and we reach the stature of the fullness of Christ. At no time in the history of the Church have we achieved those things. Therefore, based on Paul's own words, those gifts, including prophecy, are still in operation today.

How Can I Know the Will of God?

The Bible makes it very clear that God has a purpose and a plan for our lives. Any biblical scholar will agree that this did not end in the first century. But if we have a God that won't speak to us, it can be hard to discern what that plan is. Many of us have read books or heard messages on knowing the will of God. Those books are all filled with good principles that we can follow. Yet, the fact is that the Bible only gives one real principle to follow in trying to determine what is God's will for us. In the Bible when someone wanted to know the will of God, they asked Him—and He told them!

God *does* speak to His people. But if we are so entrenched in a mindset that says that God does not speak today, we can often write it off as imagination. The truth is that the prophetic is not an optional extra in the Christian life. The prophetic is not an optional extra in the Church. Amos 3:7 even goes so far as to say, "Surely the Lord GOD does nothing, unless He reveals His secret to His servants the prophets."

> Our God is constantly pouring out new revelation, continually speaking to His people. He is a God who loves us enough that He wants to enter into communication with us.

Throughout the Bible, God communicated with His people. In 1 Corinthians 12, Paul reminds the Gentiles that they once worshiped mute idols. What a foolish thing to worship something that cannot communicate! Our God, however, is not like the mute idols. Our God is constantly pouring out new revelation, continually speaking to His people. He is a God who loves us enough that He wants to enter into communication with us.

What Is Prophecy?

The definition of prophecy is simple. Prophecy is speaking the mind and heart of God as revealed by the Holy Spirit. Prophecy is the outflow of the heart and the very nature of God. Revelation 19:10 says that the testimony of Jesus is the spirit of prophecy. Jesus cares about His Church and He, therefore, has things He wants to communicate to His Church. Those communications come by way of the

Holy Spirit. That is prophecy. It is what Jesus is saying to His Church.

The testimony of Jesus, which is prophecy, is not only a corporate promise. Jesus says that His sheep know His voice (see Jn. 10:4). If you are one of His sheep, you have the capability, the capacity, and the privilege of hearing the voice of your shepherd that comes through the Holy Spirit.

Understanding the Prophets

Throughout the Bible we find several Hebrew and Greek words that are translated as "prophet." In understanding how prophecy works today, it is helpful to know the different types of prophets and prophecy taught in God's Word. Let's take a look at some of the various names the Bible uses to describe the prophets and their functions:

1. **Nabi.** This is the general Hebrew word for prophet. It means one who proclaims, announces, declares, utters communications, a spokesman, or a heralder. It is linked with the word "reveal." This word also implies a supernatural message that bubbles up or springs forth. *Nabi* is the word used in 1 Samuel 3:20, "And all Israel from Dan to Beersheba knew that Samuel had been established as a prophet of the LORD." It can be either masculine or feminine and can refer to either a prophet of God, or a false prophet who brings messages that are contrary to God's character or will.

2. **Roeh.** This Hebrew word means "seer." These prophets see the circumstances and gain revelation on how to move past it. An example is 1 Samuel 9:9, "Come, let us go to the seer." A seer is probably the most misunderstood of the prophetic types. They are the ones that have visions or visual impressions. These types of prophets can look at something and receive a supernatural message through that image. God asked many of the prophets in Scripture, "What do you see?" The Lord has often used this method of communicating with me.

3. Chozeh. This Hebrew word is translated as a seer which is akin to a watchman. According to *The New Bible Dictionary* (Tyndale House Publishers), *chozeh* was most often mentioned in association with service to the reigning king.

4. Shamar. This is another Hebrew word translated as watchman. These prophets watched after God's word and had tremendous wisdom for walking through life. Here are some examples of watchmen: "Also, I set watchmen over you, saying, 'Listen to the sound of the trumpet!'" (Jer. 6:17); "Son of man, I have made you a watchman for the house of Israel; therefore hear a word from My mouth, and give them warning from Me." A watchman sees what is coming and links it in with the promise of God, interceding until it is accomplished. In 1 Kings 18, Elijah released the word of the Lord to Ahab, which was that it would not rain for three and a half years. At the end of that time Elijah went into intercession until the he "saw" the cloud that represented God's change of seasons. Elijah was acting as a watchman who prophesied God's will, and then interceded to see it accomplished.

5. Prophetes. This Greek word signifies one who speaks for another, especially one who speaks for God. These are ones who "forthtell," which means that they speak forth a living message from God for the hour. In this context, the prophet is using interpretive gifts to forthtell the will and counsel of God. This word also signifies one who can "foretell," or give insights into future events. In this context, the prophet is using predictive gifts. This is the kind of prophet mentioned in Matthew 2:5, who wrote that the Savior would come out of the city of Bethlehem.

6. Nataph. This Hebrew word means to preach, to drop as dew from heaven, or to speak by (heavenly) inspiration. This type of prophesying is that which is generally done from a pulpit or in a public place, or a prophetic word that is given in the form of an exhortation. The word *nataph* is used in Micah 2:6, Micah 2:11, and Zechariah 13:3.

The Key to Prophecy—The Holy Spirit!

The Holy Spirit is our key to hearing God. Throughout the Bible, in both the Old and New Testaments, whenever the Holy Spirit came, prophecy flowed. Here are just a few examples: "Then the Spirit of the LORD will come upon you, and you will prophesy" (1 Sam. 10:6); "The Spirit of God came upon the messengers of Saul, and they also prophesied" (1 Sam. 19:20); "And it happened, when the Spirit rested upon them, that they prophesied" (Num. 11:25); and "And when Paul had laid hands on them, the Holy Spirit came upon them, and they spoke with tongues and prophesied" (Acts 19:6).

The Holy Spirit's ministry through prophecy did not end in the first century! In many accounts of revival throughout the Church's history, when the Holy Spirit came in power, prophecy broke lose. In fact, one of the signs of the Spirit's presence is prophecy. Through the Holy Spirit, God acts, reveals His will, empowers individuals, and reveals His personal presence. Prophecy is a key element of this process.

Why is Prophecy Important?

Prophecy is important because God tells us it is. It is just that simple. Here are three reasons we find in the Bible that help us understand God's heart toward this important gift:

1. **We are to seek to prophesy.** "Pursue love, and desire spiritual gifts, but especially that you may prophesy" (1 Cor. 14:1). In the King James Version, this verse says that we are to covet prophecy. Did you know that prophecy is the only thing in all the Bible we are supposed to covet? And what happens when we covet something? We think

about it all the time. We desire it. We think about what we could do to get it. That's how we are supposed to seek prophecy.

Revelation 2 and 3 have the words of Jesus to many different churches. Jesus gives different admonishments, different promises, and different messages to each of the seven churches listed in those passages. The one thing that does not differ from church to church, however, is Jesus' command: "He who has an ear, let him hear what the Spirit is saying." We are to hear what the Spirit is saying. We are to seek prophecy.

2. God warns us not to reject prophecy. "Do not despise prophecies. Test all things; hold fast to what is good" (1 Thes. 5:20-21). When Paul wrote to the Thessalonian church, they were still young in the Lord. They were just starting out. When something is in the beginning stages there is often a lack of maturity and a lack of understanding, which can open the door to flakiness. When flakiness springs up, there is a tendency to say that something (in this case prophecy) is more trouble than it's worth. But Paul says no. Don't shut it down. Don't quench the Spirit. Let it happen, test everything, and hold on to what is good.

The Bible also tells us not to despise tongues. The relationship between prophecy and tongues is often misunderstood. Simply put, when a tongue is interpreted, it becomes prophecy.

3. Prophecy releases the life and power of God. As we saw in Chapter One, the word of God has creative power. When Ezekiel saw the dry, dead bones, the Lord told him to prophesy to them.

"So I prophesied as I was commanded; and as I prophesied, there was a noise, and suddenly a rattling; and the bones came together, bone to bone. Indeed, as I looked, the sinews and the flesh came upon them, and the skin covered them over; but there was no breath in them. Then He said to me, 'Prophesy to the breath, prophesy, son of man, and say to the breath, 'Thus says the Lord GOD: Come from the four winds, O breath, and breathe on these slain, that they may live.'' So I prophesied as He commanded me, and breath came into them, and they lived, and stood upon their feet, an exceedingly great army" (Ezek. 37:7-10).

When the prophetic word of God goes forth, it doesn't just enlighten you or give you information-it releases life and power. Prophecy changes situations!

Understanding the Gift of Prophecy

The Holy Spirit equips us to accomplish God's purposes on earth. This is what 1 Corinthians 12, 13, and 14 are about. Too often these chapters are separated from one another in the teaching we receive. But the fact is that they were written together and they flow together to help give us an understanding of spiritual gifts and how they are to operate in the body of Christ. Let's look at this passage in light of the gift of prophecy.

The body of Christ works in just that way—it is a body, each part having a function and purpose that assists the whole in operating correctly. This is explained in some detail in 1 Corinthians 12. There are, however, certain gifts that are to be desired in the body, one of which is prophecy.

From that point, Paul immediately goes into a discourse on the evidences and importance of love. He goes so far as to say, "And though I have the gift of prophecy...but have not love, I am nothing" (1 Cor. 13:2).

From there he moves on to say, "pursue love, and desire spiritual gifts, but especially that you may prophesy" (1 Cor. 14:1). Godly prophecy cannot be separated from love. In fact, true prophecy flows from a heart of love, even if the word is one of correction. The basis for understanding the gift of prophecy is understanding issues of love.

Five Dynamic Functions of Prophecy

Having laid out a basic understanding of what prophecy is, let's now take a look at what prophecy does. From 1 Corinthians 14, we see that there are different purposes for prophecy. Here is a list of five functions that prophecy is meant to accomplish:

1. **Comfort.** To comfort is to soothe, reassure, bring cheer, bring a feeling of relief from pain or anxiety, lessen one's grief or distress, and give strength and hope by means of kindness and thoughtful attention. God is the "Father of mercies and God of all comfort, who comforts us in all our tribulation, that we may be able to comfort those who are in any trouble, with the comfort with which we ourselves are comforted by God. For as the sufferings of Christ abound in us, so our consolation also abounds through Christ" (2 Cor. 1:3-5).

God longs to comfort His hurting children. He longs to speak to them in a way that produces strength and hope. This is one of the very basic functions of prophecy that all believers should both receive and deliver to others. A prophetic word of comfort spoken at the right moment can break the back of discouragement, hopelessness, and anguish!

2. **Edification.** To edify means to instruct, benefit, uplift, enlighten, or build up. First Corinthians 14 is filled with the correlation between prophecy and edification, which is the building up of Christian character. A prophetic word, therefore, may contain elements of teaching or it may bring new revelation to our minds and spirits. The word may bring specific instruction. The word may bring a sense of strengthening a place in our lives that has been in desolation or ruins. All of these are types of edification we might receive from a prophetic

word. First Corinthians 8:1 tells us that love edifies. Because love is the basis for prophecy, all true prophecies, therefore, have an element of edification.

3. Exhortation. To exhort is to urge, advise, caution, admonish, recommend, or warn. A prophetic word that exhorts, therefore, can either build up or tear down. Exhortation may be difficult to receive. It may not be the word of comfort for which we were hoping. Even so, words of exhortation are vital in that they bring forth the ultimate purpose of God. Even a difficult word of exhortation that is delivered in the right spirit leaves us feeling a sense of relief and freedom. Prophecy should not leave us with a sense of confusion or condemnation, but rather with a sense of direction and a way of escape from bondage.

4. Redemptive. One of the basic and most beautiful functions of prophecy is seeing redemption come into lives. God's heart revealed throughout the Bible is to redeem us from the power of sin and death. Since prophecy is speaking forth the mind of God, under the inspiration of the Holy Spirit, the logical conclusion is that prophecy should be redemptive.

Several years ago, a young man named Jon received just such a word from my good friend, Cindy Jacobs. Jon was a good husband and father who was responsible and provided well for his family. He attended church every Sunday and tried his best to follow God. Yet Jon was a closet alcoholic. He was a functional alcoholic, which means that even when he was drunk, few around him knew it. Because he could handle liquor well, he was able to keep secret the fact that he could barely make it through a day without drinking. In addition, he was addicted to chewing tobacco. Yet he knew these things were wrong and had sought God for healing.

During this time in his life, he attended a weekend retreat which was being taught by Cindy. One night Jon sat quietly in the back while Cindy began giving personal words of prophecy. He felt that God would have nothing to say to him. To his amazement, Cindy pointed to him and called him forward. As he walked toward Cindy, Jon felt sure he was in trouble—as though God was going to publicly rebuke him. But as Cindy began to deliver the prophecy, he could barely believe the words! She told of how the Lord had given Jon the heart of a pastor and how He was going to use Jon in days ahead to see mighty things happen for the kingdom of God!

Jon was stunned. There was no word of rebuke. His secret life was not uncovered. Cindy had prophesied to him about his destiny rather than his addictions. The words were so powerful that Jon was completely delivered that very night from alcoholism and addiction to tobacco. Today Jon is a governing elder in his church, a cell group leader, heads an effective deliverance ministry, and is actively involved in implementing city-taking strategies where he lives. Jon will tell you that the turning point in his life was the night when God showed him his redemptive purpose rather than condemning him for his shortcomings. That is redemptive prophecy in action!

5. Direction. As we see throughout the Bible, prophets are given to bring direction to God's people. I have known my coauthor, Rebecca Sytsema, for many years. In the early '90s we both served on Cindy Jacobs' staff at Generals of Intercession. During that time, Rebecca went through a two-year period of intensive healing in her life over many issues. I knew that the healing process had brought her to a place where she was ready for marriage. In early 1994, we were preparing to go to a conference in California. One day I looked at her and said, "You need to be at that conference. God has your husband waiting there!"

My words confirmed a feeling that she had been having for about a week, but she had not made her hotel reservations. I immediately picked up the phone and called the hotel where the rest of us were staying. I was told there were no rooms left. I simply told the woman on the phone that first of all Rebecca's father, Peter Wagner, was in charge of the conference, and secondly, her husband would be waiting for her there. The woman on the phone checked again and found one room left. It was at that conference that Rebecca met Jack Sytsema, God's perfect match for her. Two years later I had the privilege of performing their wedding.

This is a case in which God gave a clear word of direction and then made a way to see His prophesied will come to pass.

The Process of Prophecy

Besides the functions of prophecy, it is important to understand the process of prophecy—that is, how it works in our lives on an ongoing basis. Here are three important elements of the process of prophecy in our lives:

1. **Prophecy is progressive.** "For we know in part and we prophesy in part" (1 Cor. 13:9). No personal or corporate word of prophecy is complete in and of itself. In his excellent book, *Developing Your Prophetic Gifting*, Graham Cooke says, "God only reveals what we need to know in order to do his will in that particular time and place. The things that he does not wish us to know, he keeps secret from the one prophesying. Elisha said, 'The Lord has hidden it from me!' (2 Kings 4:27). In other words, 'I don't know.'"[1]

God may give us a little bit here and a little bit there. In retrospect, we may wonder why God didn't tell us this or that, or why He did tell us some seemingly unimportant detail. God always knows what He is doing when He reveals His heart to us through prophecy. That is something that we must simply trust. We must bear in mind, however, that we do not know all we may encounter, or how the prophecies may be fulfilled. Prophecy may point out a path, but we must follow the Lord daily and trust in Him as we move ahead along that path.

2. Prophecy evolves. As we follow the Lord in obedience, He will give us our next piece. He will not tell us what He wants us to do three steps down the road. He gives it to us step-by-step. Such was the case with Abraham. God gave him a piece here and a piece there. Each time Abraham obeyed, God would speak to him again until He brought him into the fullness of what He wanted him to do. God would confirm, expand, give new insights and move Abraham on to his next place.

That is the way of prophecy. Each prophetic word is incomplete, yet as we are faithful to obey God, we receive new pieces of the puzzle. Prophecies will build on earlier prophecies to bring confirmation and fresh understanding.

3. Prophecy is provisional. The key to the process of prophecy is obedience. God will not usurp our wills and force us to follow His will. Mary, for instance, could have said no to the prophetic pronouncement that she would become pregnant. Instead, she responded by saying, "Behold the maidservant of the Lord! Let it be to me according to your word" (Luke 1:38). Had she said no, the Holy Spirit would never have forced her to become pregnant! Although she did not completely understand how this would happen, nor did she probably grasp the magnitude of that for which she had been chosen, nevertheless, she knew that through the prophetic word God had revealed His destiny for her life. Through her choice of obedience, the word came to pass and the human race has been blessed ever since.

The Value of Prophecy

Prophecy is a tremendous gift that God has given to His Church. It is full of tremendous benefits for us, both individually and corporately. Here is a list of some of the values of receiving this gift into our lives and churches:

1. **Prophecy brings healing.** Proverbs 25:11 says, "A word fitly spoken is like apples of gold in settings of silver." Accepting the comfort and edification available through prophecy can heal a broken heart. As Graham Cooke writes, "Hurts, wounds, rejections and emotional trauma are a part of our lives, both before and after salvation. The Good News is that we serve a God who is committed to our healing at every level (physical, mental, and emotional). The goal of God is wholeness of life and fullness of the Spirit. Prophecy is a wonderful part of that healing and renewing process. Prophecy brings us, by direct verbal communication, into contact with God's real perspective on our lives and current situations." [2]

2. **Prophecy deepens our relationship with God.** When we ponder how the God of all creation cares enough to send a personal message from His heart, no matter what the function of the prophecy, it causes us to stop and think about what our individual value to Him must be! Receiving His word brings a new appreciation of God's deep love and care for us. It reminds us of our position with Him. As in any relationship, communication is a key to reaching deeper levels. When God communicates with us, and we respond to Him, our relationship becomes deeper and more meaningful.

3. **Prophecy provides direction and renewed vision.** When we receive God's word, we often get a clearer understanding of where He is leading us. Knowing where we are headed causes us to focus more intently on the plans and goals God has for us. New excitement and vision are often direct results of the prophetic word that brings us direction.

4. **Prophecy brings biblical insight.** As we will see in the next chapter, prophecy must line up with the written Word of God. That being the case, the revelation that comes through prophecy will often open up new insights and inspire deeper understanding of mysteries in the Bible. Paul says that we can gain "knowledge in the mystery of

Christ which in other ages was not made known to the sons of men, as it has now been revealed by the Spirit to His holy apostles and prophets" (Eph. 3:4-5). Prophecy will often serve as a catalyst for understanding biblical truths that we have not seen or understood before.

5. **Prophecy confirms.** God has a number of ways He uses to communicate with us. It may come through reading Scripture or hearing a message or counseling with a friend. God delights in confirming His message to us. He will often use prophecy to say something to us that we may have heard in some other form.

6. **Prophecy can warn.** God does not want us ensnared by our own sin or by schemes of the devil. Prophecy, delivered in love, can often warn us that our own sin will result in calamity and despair down the road if we do not repent and turn to God. Prophecy can also warn us of traps the enemy has set for us. After the birth of Jesus, the wise men were warned not to return to Herod (Matt. 2:12). Then Mary and Joseph were prophetically warned to flee to Egypt and stay there until the Lord spoke to them again in order to spare Jesus from Herod's plot to kill Him (Matt. 2:13). Paul was warned by Jesus in Acts 22:18, "Make haste and get out of Jerusalem quickly, for they will not receive your testimony concerning Me." Because God sees the destiny He has for us, He often uses the prophetic word to warn us of the snares the enemy has set up to destroy our destined purposes.

7. **Prophecy can bring salvation.** As I mentioned in chapter one, when I was 11 years old, I clearly heard the voice of the Lord say, "This is your day." That was the day of my salvation. All salvation is a result of hearing the voice of the Lord on some level. Yet there are times when the Lord clearly speaks. Graham Cooke writes, "I have seen many atheists and agnostics persuaded by God through prophecy. It is the work of the Spirit to convict of sin (John 16:8-11). Prophecy can uncover past history which needs to be amended. It can provide an agenda for repentance, restitution, and revival." [3]

8. Prophecy releases new practices into the Church. There is nothing new under the sun, but there are diverse administrations. The administration of the 13th century will not work in the 21st century. By "new practices," I do not mean a departure from the Apostles' Creed. But there are new methods of operation and administration that God is revealing to the Church that will burst us forth into new practices and new strategies that will work for the 21st century. Life means movement, so the minute we stop moving forward, we run the risk of facing death. Therefore, one of Satan's greatest strategies is to get us caught up in yesterday's methods. Prophecy breaks us out of the old and into the new methods that are relevant for today.

9. Prophecy provides insight into counseling. When I am involved in a counseling situation, I rely on the prophetic voice of God to provide me with the understanding I need to give godly wisdom. The Lord will often reveal to me what the problem is, what the root is, and give me a prophetic word to unlock the strategy that the person needs to move forward in God's plan for their life. It has proven to be a very effective method of counseling.

10. Prophecy shows us how to pray. There are times when our prayer lives can be stalled. When we know the will of God in a certain area, we have great fuel for our prayer lives. God's will is made known to us through the prophetic. That knowledge gives us a basis for ongoing prayer to see His will done on earth as it is in heaven.

11. Prophecy releases strategy for warfare. Praying through a prophetic word can often entail spiritual warfare. Timothy 1:18 says, "This charge I commit to you, son Timothy, according to the prophecies previously made concerning you, that by them you may wage the good warfare." Joshua also received prophetic instruction on the warfare he was to wage in order to see the walls of Jericho fall (Josh. 6:1-5). Many times we see the enemy but we don't know how to wait for

God's strategy to come. Prophecy can provide us with the strategy we need to war against the enemy who strives to keep God's plans from manifesting in our lives. We can often gain wisdom for knowing how to war.

12. Prophecy stirs faith. Prophecy can change things. When our spirits receive a word from the Lord, we know that there is hope, that there is a way to see that prophetic word fulfilled. Remember how Jon was freed from alcoholism when Cindy gave him a redemptive prophecy? Jon's faith for seeing God deliver him and bring him into his destiny skyrocketed that day! That is the power of prophecy. In the next chapter we will discuss the relationship between prophecy and faith in greater detail.

Ezekiel and the Four Steps to Fulfillment

We must be in a perpetual process of receiving prophetic revelation. Our life and destiny is on a continuum. As we move through life, we need to constantly seek new direction and new revelation from God. We can't just grab a hold of one level of revelation and think that's going to ride us through to the end. In our book *The Best is Yet Ahead*, Rebecca and I explain the four levels of prophecy that we can see working in the life of Ezekiel in his vision of the Valley of Dry Bones. If Ezekiel had stopped at any point before God's full purpose had been accomplished, he would have failed. Ezekiel went through a four-step process at each new level of prophecy. These four steps are the same ones we need to follow if we are going to stay on track with prophetic fulfillment in our own lives:

Step One: He received prophetic revelation. Ezekiel sought God and was open to receiving prophetic instruction. In fact, he *expected* God to speak to him. How often in our daily lives do we *expect* to hear God? God is speaking to us today! We need to learn how to listen for God's voice and direction in our lives in order to receive the instructions that will move us forward.

Step Two: He obeyed the voice of the Lord. God told Ezekiel what to say and do in order for the next step to be accomplished. This seems so basic, and yet it is a critical step that we must understand. Ezekiel could not have moved to the complete fulfillment of prophecy without first obeying God at the first, second, and third levels. If you are having difficulty gaining new revelation and hearing the voice of the Lord, go back and be sure you have done all that the Lord has required of you thus far. For example, if you have fallen out of relationship with someone, and the Lord reveals to you that you need to go get right with that person, you should not go back to the Lord looking for new revelation until you have obeyed Him in the last revelation. If you want to continue to move forward toward prophetic fulfillment, you need to go get right with that person.

Step Three: He watched God's purpose being accomplished and assessed the situation. At each level of obedience, Ezekiel saw miracles happen as God's will was accomplished. Even so, he knew that all of God's purposes had not yet been fulfilled. He saw the bones come together. This in itself must have been a great and miraculous sight. But when he looked closer, he saw that even with this great miracle, there was no breath. Then he saw breath come into them. A great army of living, breathing beings replaced a dead pile of dry, useless bones. And yet there was hopelessness and infirmity. It was not until Ezekiel saw the Lord break infirmity and death off of the great army and bring them into the land He had promised them that the process of prophetic fulfillment was complete. Even though we may see great miracles along the way, we need to be sensitive to the Holy Spirit's leading as to whether or not His will has been fully accomplished.

Step Four: He listened for his next instruction. Miracle after miracle did not stop Ezekiel from seeking God for the next step. He did not bask in the awesome works of God in a way that stopped Him from looking forward. Of course we need to stop and thank God for His great power and allow ourselves to be drawn into worship. But, we can't let the glory of something that has already occurred keep us from moving toward a greater level of glory.

Notes
[1] Graham Cooke, *Developing Your Prophetic Gifting* (Kent, England: Sovereign World, Ltd., 1994), p. 119.
[2] Ibid., pp. 30-31.
[3] Ibid., pp. 39-40.

CHAPTER THREE

Receiving the
Word of the Lord:
Testing and Responding
to a Prophetic Word

T here are many ways we can receive a prophetic word from the
Lord. We may have an impression in our spirit, or the Lord may
illuminate a passage of Scripture that has particular significance in our
lives, or we may have a vivid, prophetic dream. Prophecy can also
come when someone is communicating wisdom and counsel that gives
you the direction you are looking for in your life. Someone may even
say, "I believe the Spirit of God is saying this to you." Prophecy can
also come by God or angelic beings visiting you and giving supernatural revelation. These are all sound, biblical methods which God uses
at different times to speak to us.

Prophecy Has Boundaries

There are several things we must be aware of as we begin to move into receiving prophetic words. We must understand that prophecy has boundaries that God has established for our own protection. For instance, in a corporate setting, Paul gives the following guideline: "Let two or three prophets speak, and let the others judge" (1 Cor. 14:29). Another boundary is set in 1 Thessalonians 5:19-21, "Do not quench the Spirit. Do not despise prophecies. Test all things; hold fast to what is good." The rest of this chapter is devoted to applying tests to prophetic words so that we can hold fast to what is good.

Is My Word From God?

Not every voice we hear is from the Holy Spirit. Satan has the ability to counterfeit gifts in order to bring confusion and get us off course. His ability to counterfeit includes the gift of prophecy. Jeremiah records the Lord saying, "I have not sent these prophets, yet they ran. I have not spoken to them, yet they prophesied" (Jer. 23:21).

That still happens. There are false prophets. That is why we are admonished to test all things and hold onto what is good. Here are some unclean sources of prophetic words that we need to be aware of:

1. The occult. "You are wearied in the multitude of your counsels; let now the astrologers, the stargazers, and the monthly prognosticators stand up and save you from what shall come upon you" (Isa. 47:13). Occultic sources of prophecy include psychics, tarot cards, Ouija boards, astrology and horoscopes, clairvoyants, mediums, ESP, witchcraft, divination, and so forth. These sources of prophetic utterance must be avoided completely! Saul, for example, gained revelation by visiting a witch. However, because it was an illegitimate source of revelation, not from God, it ultimately resulted in Saul's death.

2. Delusions. "How long will this be in the heart of the prophets who prophesy lies? Indeed they are prophets of the deceit of their own heart" (Jer. 23:26). Not everyone that gives you a false prophecy is malicious; they are just confused. Sometimes they are walking in their own delusion, thinking they are hearing God when they are not.

3. Unrestrained desires. Desires are a natural function of the human emotion. Desires are linked with our wishes, aspirations, urges, and expectations. Gone unchecked, desires can cause us to rebel against the will of God in our lives. Have you ever heard anyone use the expression, "yearning desire?" Many times we can so yearn to have something that we will listen for any voice that will align with our desires. False prophecy can, therefore, come through a desire so unrestrained that we can no longer discern the voice of the Lord over the voice of the enemy or our own flesh. Prophecy can come out of the longings of someone's heart, rather than from a pure word from the Lord.

4. Manipulation and control. "Likewise, son of man, set your face against the daughters of your people, who prophesy out of their own heart; prophesy against them" (Ezek. 13:17). Prophecy has been used to try and manipulate people into actions they may not otherwise take. For instance, someone might want this person to marry that person. It seems like a good thing-so good, in fact, that God must want it too, so they may go up to one or the other and say, "The Lord says you are to marry _____." The true origin behind the word was not God, but a manipulative and controlling spirit. We will discuss this more later in the chapter.

5. Immaturity. There are true prophets that have not yet matured in their gifting that may deliver a word from the Lord mixed with their own emotions. Therefore, the word is impure. This is where some sifting needs to take place, and we are to "hold fast to what is good."

6. False dreams. "Behold, I am against those who prophesy false dreams" (Jer. 23:32). The enemy is able to counterfeit prophetic dreams, just as he is able to counterfeit prophetic words. We must realize that when we are asleep, we are not fully active in our spirit. Many times the enemy will use this time to speak false words to us.

7. **Demons.** "And I have seen folly in the prophets of Samaria: they prophesied by Baal and caused My people Israel to err" (Jer. 23:13). Just as the Lord can send angels to prophesy, the enemy can also send one of his hosts (Baal was sent in the biblical example given) to deliver a demonic prophecy.

Judging Prophecy

There are many origins for what may seem like prophecy from God. So how do you know if what is being said is from God? How do we test prophecy? Here is a list that has been compiled partly from Graham Cooke's *Developing Your Prophetic Gifting,* along with my own experience in judging prophecy:

1. **Does the word you have received edify, exhort, and comfort you?** Does it accomplish the basic functions we outlined in the last chapter? 1 Corinthians 14:3 says that the real purpose of prophecy is to edify, exhort, and comfort. If the word leaves you with a sense of uneasiness instead of edification, or you feel that something is just not right, you should not receive the word without further testing.

2. **What is the spirit behind the prophecy?** Someone might begin to speak a word to you, but the spirit behind the word does not seem right. It may have a spirit of condemnation on it. Even though it could be totally true, if you feel weighed down and condemned, you may need to judge it further. Remember, the spirit in which all prophecy should be given is love. Therefore, even a word of exhortation or correction should leave you with a freedom to rebuild.

3. **Does it conform to Scripture?** God is not going to say one thing in the Bible and then tell you the opposite in a prophetic word. The prophetic word of the Lord will *always* line up with the inspired, written Word of God that has been given to us as a guide and an ex-

ample. Remember, the Bible has no bounds or time frame; therefore, you will find that the principles and the illumination of the Word of God are just as important for us today as it was when it was written. In other words, your example or scriptural principle may be found in the Old Testament as often as in the New Testament. But if someone gives you a word and you find no scriptural principle, basis, or example for that word in the Bible, please do not fully embrace the word.

4. Does it display the character of Christ? In her book, *The Voice of God*, Cindy Jacobs says, "Sometimes wolves in sheep's clothing manipulate Scripture for their own purposes. Just because someone is quoting chapter and verse to you doesn't make a prophecy accurate. Even if Scripture is being used, another area to check is to make sure Christ's character shines through the prophetic word." [1] This, again, leads to love. In addition to love, prophetic words should also exalt Jesus rather than a person or ministry. They should lead us to His feet rather than to an organization.

5. Is it manipulative or controlling? Even though some words are filled with truth, they can manipulate or control a person under the desire of the one giving the word. Control and manipulation are used to wield power, abuse, dominate, or rule over others. Such a word has no love, much less any of the other fruit of the spirit, and should be discarded.

6. Does it usurp your will? Does the word say you *must* do this or that? Does it overpower you in such a way that you are not able to exercise your own free will to choose what you will do? If so, there should be a red flag. God gives us all freedom—even the freedom to sin. All prophetic words should leave you the choice to either accept them or reject them.

7. Does it pull rank? In other words, does the word begin to move you out of the authority structure in which God has placed you? Does it breed rebellion against authority, produce suspicion or insubordination? Does it pull you out of the place God has you spiritually? God gave each of His children an authority structure in which to operate. If the word suggests that you supercede biblical authority, reject it!

8. Does it confirm what God is saying to you? God is always willing to confirm His word to us. When God gives a word, He will usually give it over and over again in many forms. Prophetic words often confirm what God has already spoken to you, and fit in with what He is doing in your life.

9. Does it allow outside perspective? If someone gives you a word and says that you are not supposed to communicate it with anyone else, be careful. That is a violation of Scripture. Remember that 1 Thessalonians tells us that any word of God is to be evaluated. Godly council is always in order, particularly when the word tells you something drastic, like quit your job and move to another city. Proverbs tells us there is wisdom in a multitude of counselors, and that includes judging the prophetic. In fact, a good test of any prophecy is to take it to a mature spiritual friend or authority in your life and ask them to help you judge the word.

> A good test of any prophecy is to take it to a mature spiritual friend or authority in your life and ask them to help you judge the word.

10. Does it give a dire warning? Warnings are fine, but see what kind of a warning it is. Is the warning so dire that you have no way out and it produces hopelessness in you, or does the warning show you your way of escape? Is there redemption?

Cindy Jacobs tells the story of one such warning that I prophesied over Houston, Texas, on September 21, 1994. The word was, "'*I would say, the next 24 days are critical.* Though the enemy has stood against you as a city, I have brought you to a crossroads and you are about to make a transition and crossover. My eyes are upon this city and the remnant of this city, and I will overcome the structures that are set against My Spirit in this city. Revelation that has been withheld is going to begin to come down to people like rain. *Look to the river of the east.* As that river rises so will My people.'

"'…Watchman, what do you see?' He replied, '*I see a fire. It is a literal fire. Fire is on the river.'* Then the Lord said, 'My fire will begin to come to this city.'

"'I would call you to the night watch. Gather together in the night watch. Sing in the night in the hard areas of the city and evil will be uncovered and deliverance will come. If you will enter into the night watch, you will overthrow the impending destruction and doom that is set for the area.'

"One of the prayer leaders, Deborah DeGar, took the prophetic word from church to church, leading a prayer watch from 3:00-6:00 a.m. *At the end of 24 days, it began to rain in Houston.* There had never been a flood exactly like it in the history of the city. Houston was brought before the eyes of the nation. The San Jacinto River *(the river to the east)* began to rise and flood the entire territory. Gas lines erupted underneath the river and the flooded river *literally had a fire that burned in its midst.* In the middle of the chaos, the Church came together in great unity.

"In the case of this prophetic warning, the flooding was not averted, but it did not do the damage it could have done." [2]

11. How do I feel about the word in my spirit? God has given each of us discernment in our spirits. If we receive a prophetic word, and it just doesn't seem right to us, for whatever reason, we have cause to check it out further before we embrace it as a word from the Lord.

12. Is it confirmed by the church? If a word is given in a corporate setting, there should be instant feedback from the people and the leaders. There should be a corporate "amen" that comes forth. Rebecca Sytsema, my coauthor, was once in a meeting in the Anaheim Vineyard when a man stood up during worship to give a prophetic word. He said that the Lord was longing to fulfill the desire of His children's hearts. He said that God was, in fact, a God who longed to bring even what seems like fairy tales to pass. He finished his word and sat down. When worship concluded, John Wimber came to the microphone. After a moment of silence, he simply stated, "Our God is *not* a fairy tale God!" A loud round of applause went up from the crowd, many of whom had discerned that something had not been right with the word. If a word was given in a corporate setting, what was the reaction of the leaders and the congregation?

13. Does it come to pass? "When a prophet speaks in the name of the LORD, if the thing does not happen or come to pass, that is the thing which the LORD has not spoken; the prophet has spoken it presumptuously" (Deut. 18:22). Here is, of course, one of the most basic tests of a prophetic word. Remember, prophecy may be conditional, based on something we must do. If you read through the list of responses below, and are satisfied that you have done all that God has required of you concerning the word, and it is still not fulfilled, it may not have been a word from the Lord at all.

14. Does it produce fruit? A true word from the Lord will bear good fruit that we will be able to discern. In his book *Prophecy*, Bruce Yocum writes, "If we pay attention to the effect that prophetic utterances have, we can judge their worth. A word from the Lord will produce life, peace, hope, love, and all the other fruit of the Holy Spirit. A word which is not from the Lord will either produce the fruit of evil—strife, anger, jealousy, lust, indifference—or it will have no effect at all." [3] What kind of fruit has the prophetic word given to you produced in your life? This will be a telling factor in whether or not you accept it as a word from the Lord.

Responding to Prophecy

Once we have tested a prophetic word and have come to the conclusion that God has spoken into our lives, we must then understand how to respond to what we have been told. Here is a helpful checklist of proper actions to take:

1. **Keep a journal.** There is tremendous importance in writing down, tape recording, or keeping some kind of record of prophetic words. Don't rely purely on your memory. Having a record of prophecy helps us to remember the whole word, keeps us from adding thoughts to the word, and builds our faith when we go back and read the word. We can also see how the word we receive fits in with what God has said to us in the past.

There are times, however, when we do not clearly understand all that God is trying to say to us at the time the word is given. Having a record of the word helps us go back and gain fresh understanding at a later time. For example, in June of 1998, I was given a birthday party at the home of C. Peter Wagner. Cindy Jacobs had come to help celebrate. During the party, Cindy began feeling a spirit of prophecy come upon her. Peter, who keeps a full prophetic journal, grabbed a tape recorder. Cindy gave me a beautiful word for the new year I was entering into in my own life. Then she turned to Peter and began to prophesy that God was calling him to raise up a seminary that would gather leaders from around the world. She went on to give several specific details.

At the time such a thought had never entered Peter's mind. He had no frame of reference for such a concept. Nonetheless, Cindy's word was transcribed and entered on page 67 of the Wagner Prophetic Journal. A few months later Peter met with several apostles from various streams of Christianity. During that meeting, the Lord spoke to Peter about a whole new concept for training leaders from around the world. It became clear that he was to retire from his position as a professor at Fuller Theological Seminary, where he had taught for 30 years, and begin his own seminary-type school. As he obeyed the Lord, God began pouring new revelation out as to how the school would operate. Later that year, he officially formed Wagner Leadership Institute, and the first student was enrolled that December.

Peter was able to go back to page 67 of his journal and revisit exactly what the Lord had spoken to him. In fact, as he began to seek counsel and set up the leadership for the school, he was able to distribute copies of the word Cindy had given him so that those involved would also know the word God had given over the new venture.

2. Do not interpret the word by the desires of your flesh. Many of God's people have fallen into deception by taking a prophetic word and adding their own interpretation to it, then saying that God promised them this or that. Cindy Jacobs offers the following caution: "I have had many singles come to me saying God has promised them certain mates because they were told so in prophecies. When I asked them what the prophecies said, they came up with something like, 'God said He would give me the desires of my heart and so-and-so is the desire of my heart.' (Such an interpretation) may be the desire of their flesh but God may not have anything to do with it at all."[4] Be very careful not to take a word and run in a direction God has not ordained.

3. Embrace the word. To embrace means to grab hold of something. When we embrace or grab hold of a word, it activates faith to see the word fulfilled. Remember that faith comes by hearing and hearing by the word of God (Rom. 10:17). When we embrace a true prophetic word, it brings faith that God has a destiny for us. We must allow ourselves to embrace our prophetic word with the faith that God is well able to do what He said He would do. If God has inspired the word, He will uphold it by the Holy Spirit. Even if we have received a difficult word, if the word is from God, faith will rise within our spirit because we know that God has a path for us.

When I was 18, the Lord spoke to me and said, "I have called you for the healing of the nations." At that time the only frame of reference I had for a call to the nations was to become a missionary, which was something I did not want to do. Even though I was willing to obey God, I did not embrace His word to me. It was 10 years later when God spoke that word to me again. This time I embraced the word fully. He then began to show me that He had not called me to be a missionary, but rather an intercessor, prophet, and strategist for the nations He would lay on my heart. He began to open doors for me to travel in and out of nations so that I could bring prophetic words and build up strategic intercession to see His will accomplished. Had I not been willing to embrace this word when He spoke it to me for a second time, I would have missed that portion of His destiny for my life.

4. **Pray it through.** Because prophecy is provisional, once we know what God wants to do in our lives, the best thing to do is to begin to pray along those lines. This will not only help to build our relationship to God and build persistence in faith, it can also teach us spiritual warfare. The enemy does not want to see God's will accomplished in our lives and will do all he can to see that we are not successful in reaching our destinies. That is why we must commit ourselves to praying through the word until we see it come to pass. For instance, I have known many barren couples who have received words about children. Yet they did not conceive immediately. In some cases, it took

years. But as they chose to pray through their word with the faith that God is well able to do all that He says, the bondage of barrenness broke off not only their physical bodies, but often their spiritual lives as well.

5. Obey the word. As we mentioned in chapter three, prophecy is often provisional. That means that there is something we must do to see it come to pass. There are conditions to meet. Here is a good biblical example: *"If* My people who are called by My name will humble themselves, and pray and seek My face, and turn from their wicked ways, *then* I will hear from heaven, and will forgive their sin and heal their land" (2 Chron. 7:14, italics added). Does God want to forgive the sin and heal the land of His people? Of course! But they have something they must do in order to see that prophecy occur, namely, humble themselves, pray, seek His face, and turn from their wicked ways. Something that has been prophesied to us may never come to pass if we are not faithful to meet the conditions.

In chapter three I told the story of how Rebecca was to go to the conference in order to meet Jack. Had she not gone to that conference, she could have missed meeting God's chosen mate. God surely could have arranged another way for them to meet, but there was a timing issue involved as well. Her obedience to the prophetic word kept her moving forward in God's timing and destiny for her life.

6. Look for the fulfillment of the word. Having completed steps one through five, we should look for and expect that the word will be fulfilled. John 1:14 speaks of the word becoming flesh. That is a good statement for the fulfillment of a prophetic word. God desires that His word be made flesh—that the intangible substance of a prophetic promise become a tangible reality in our lives. Many do not see their promise manifested because they do not know how to "watch" for the fulfillment of their word.

Can I Prophesy?

While it is not within the scope of this book to thoroughly answer this question, the discussion of prophecy would not be complete without a brief look at who can prophesy. While not all of us are called as God's spokespersons on the earth, the fact is that we all prophesy, whether it is through sharing an encouraging word, edifying a friend, giving godly advice, or knowingly giving a prophetic word. Romans 12:6 says we prophesy according to our measure of faith. What measure of faith are you operating in? I want to encourage you to ask God right now to increase your faith.

If you are a believer in the Lord Jesus Christ, the Holy Spirit is made resident within you. You can now ask the Spirit of God to begin to speak through you, knowing that He can. You can also give Him liberty to begin to manifest His particular giftings within you, whether they are prophecy, helps, hospitality, teaching, or any of the gifts listed in Romans 12, 1 Corinthians 12, and Ephesians 4. All the gifts are greatly needed in the body of Christ-including yours!

Notes
[1] Cindy Jacobs, *The Voice of God* (Ventura, CA: Regal Books, 1995), p. 76.
[2] Ibid., p. 181.
[3] Bruce Yocum, *Prophecy* (Ann Arbor, MI: Word of Life, 1976), p. 119.
[4] Jacobs, Op Cit., pp. 83-84.

CHAPTER FOUR

Walking in Revelation

"That the God of our Lord Jesus Christ, the Father of glory, may give to you the spirit of wisdom and revelation in the knowledge of Him, the eyes of your understanding being enlightened; that you may know what is the hope of His calling, what are the riches of the glory of His inheritance in the saints"
(Eph. 1:17-18).

When God speaks to us, whether by prophecy or any number of other means, His purpose in so doing is to bring a new level of revelation to our lives. Revelation is essential for living a victorious Christian life. We need the spirit of wisdom and revelation in order to accomplish the hope of God's calling over our lives. We need God not only to reveal what our next step should be, we also need Him to reveal the snares the enemy has set for us on the road ahead so that we can walk in wisdom.

Revelation means to manifest, to make clear, to show forth, to unfold, to explain by narration, to instruct, to admonish, to warn, or to give an answer to a question. When God speaks to us, He brings one or more of these aspects of revelation so that the "eyes of our minds may be enlightened" to who He is. Throughout the Bible, God actively disclosed Himself to humanity. God has not wavered in His desire that we understand Him as well. He continues to reveal His power, His glory, His nature, His character, His will, His ways, His plans, and His strategies to His people today.

Revelation from God has three important functions in our lives. They are:

1. **Revelation causes obscure things to become clear.** Jeremiah 33:3 in the Amplified Version says, "Call to Me and I will answer you and show you great and mighty things, fenced in and hidden, which you do not know (do not distinguish and recognize, have knowledge of and understand)."

2. **Revelation brings hidden things to light.** One important definition of revelation is *apocalypse*, which means to unveil or reveal something that is hidden so that it may be seen and known for what it is. We need this kind of revelation in our lives to understand how to overcome Satan's attempts to thwart God's plan for our lives.

3. **Revelation shows signs that will point us into our path of destiny.** We need revelation in order to know God's will for our lives and, as we come into agreement with His will, how to walk it out. By this we see that revelation is not a one time deal. We need fresh revelation on a continual basis to keep moving forward in God's plan and timing.

Gaining Revelation

These three functions of revelation help us understand the "why," but an even bigger question is "how." To answer that question, let's look at Ephesians 1:20-23:

"...which He worked in Christ when He raised Him from the dead and seated Him at His right hand in the heavenly places, far above all principality and power and might and dominion, and every name that is named, not only in this age but also in that which is to come. And He put all things under His feet, and gave Him to be head over all things to the church, which is His body, the fullness of Him who fills all in all."

This passage tells us that Jesus is able to defeat the enemy's structures in our lives from His position as Head because all things are under His feet. Because Jesus is Head, we need to think the way He thinks, and put on the mind of Christ (see 1 Cor. 2:16). Our cognitive processes must align with the thoughts of God in order to be successful in the earth realm.

The problem is that our minds are naturally at enmity with God because of our flesh. We must find a way, therefore, to go beyond our brains and move to a place where we have put on the mind of Christ and where the Spirit of wisdom and revelation has been activated in our lives. To do this, we need to move into that realm of faith where God will be able to show us new revelation in a way that we, as individuals, can receive. The first important step in gaining revelation, therefore, is believing that God has revelation for us and that He has a way to communicate it to us. The next step is being open and aware of what God is saying. The third step is to enter into a new realm of faith.

Faith Comes By Hearing, and Hearing by the Word of God!

Faith is the general persuasion of the mind that a certain statement is true. The primary idea behind faith is trust. When we believe that something is true, it is worthy of our trust. Romans 12:16-17 says, "But they have not all obeyed the gospel. For Isaiah says, 'Lord, who has believed our report?' So then faith comes by hearing, and hearing by the word of God."

The Holy Spirit uses the Word of God to awaken a response of faith within us. Our trust in the Word of God is the stable ground on which we stand for salvation. A response of faith produces certain characteristics within us. Here is a list of the characteristics of faith and the opposite of each one of faith's qualities:

TRUST vs. MISTRUST

BELIEF vs. UNBELIEF

LOYALTY vs. BETRAYAL

FIDELITY vs. UNFAITHFULNESS

CONFIDENCE vs. INSECURITY

OBEDIENCE vs. DISOBEDIENCE

WHOLENESS vs. FRAGMENTATION

When I hear a word from the Lord or the voice of the Spirit of God quickening His voice within me, I weigh that voice based on the characteristics of faith. When I hear a voice that represents the opposite of faith to me, I reject that voice. God has given us each a measure of faith. Romans 12:6 says, "If we prophesy, let us prophesy in proportion to our faith." Our faith should be ever growing and becoming stronger.

The concept of faith is the keynote central Christian message. Based upon our faith, we enter into the state of salvation (Eph. 2:8-9). Our sanctification is linked to faith (Acts 26:18). Our continuing purification is a result of our faith (Acts 15:9). We are justified by faith (Rom. 4:5; 5:1). Thank the Lord that we are adopted and through faith we gain a supernatural faith structure (Rom. 8:15, Gal. 3:26). Faith is also called a fruit of the spirit. Fruit is something that can be created and seen in a person (Gal. 5:22). Faith is also a supernatural gift that gives us the ability to do great acts for God. Jesus said we could "move mountains" (Matt. 17:20, 1 Cor. 13:2).

An Example Using Scripture

As we said earlier, the primary way God speaks to us on a regular basis is through Scripture. He may use a verse or passage to bring great revelation for a specific situation in your life. But not everyone who reads the Bible gains revelation. Some read it purely for historical value. Others read it in the same way they would a Chinese proverb—for principles and insight, but nothing more. However, a Christian, in whom the Spirit of God is alive and active, can read the same passages and gain incredible, tremendous insight, and hear the *now* voice of God for their lives.

There are four Greek words used to describe the functions of the Word of God. These four words describe how different individuals can read the same passage of Scripture and each walk away having received something different:

1. *graphe* – This is the written, historical Word of God. Anyone, saved or not, can read and understand the Bible from this perspective. Reading the Bible as *graphe* would be like reading a novel. You understand the story and possibly even the historical value, maybe ponder the characters and settings, but really glean little else.

2. *logos* – This is coming to see the meaning of the principles of the Bible. This would include understanding the personal value of following the golden rule or reaping what has been sown. These are generally good life principles to follow, but again, can be of value whether saved or unsaved.

3. *rhema* – This is where the Word of God crosses over into revelation. *Rhema* is when the *graphe* and *logos* are illuminated to

you by the Holy Spirit. *Rhema* brings enlightenment and bears witness in your spirit. No one who is truly saved has been so without a *rhema* understanding of their need for Christ in their lives.

4. *zoe* – All Christians have received a *rhema* word from God, or they could not have come into salvation. For some, their revelation from God ends there. However, for those who walk in the Spirit of wisdom and revelation, reading the Word of God becomes a creative, living part of who they are. When the Word of God becomes *zoe*, it dwells within you. The *rhema* becomes sustained, life-giving revelation. God has clear channels to speak revelation to those who read the Bible as *zoe* life.

Having looked at the different functions of the Bible, let's look at one way to move from reading the Bible as *graphe* to gaining *zoe* revelation. Let's take Jeremiah 33:3 as an example, which we have already quoted. Take the Scripture and read it out loud. Then write the Scripture out, outlining the main points. For example:

a.   call to Me

b.   I will answer you

c.   show you great and mighty things fenced in and hidden

Then ask God to activate the spirit of wisdom and revelation in you regarding that passage. Ask Him to show you things that go beyond your brain; things that you do not currently distinguish or recognize. Ask Him to show you things that you have not seen before. Write down any and all impressions you receive as you are meditating on the Scripture. You may want to do this on more than one occasion. As you allow yourself to receive these impressions, and trust the impressions enough to write them down, allow faith that God is speaking to you to arise within you. When it begins to become alive, and you start seeing *rhema* revelation that you have not seen before, then ask God how that applies to you and your situation. Ask Him to establish the *rhema* within you, so that it becomes ongoing, sustained *zoe* life.

Of course, there are many ways to hear God, and God may bring us *zoe* revelation without going through this process. But for those who are not used to receiving revelation from God, this simple formula is one place to start.

Some Ways God Speaks

Hearing the voice of God and receiving revelation is not as difficult as some might think. Many of God's people are hearing Him, but have not learned to perceive His voice. As we have said before, to perceive means to take hold of, feel, comprehend, grasp mentally, recognize, observe or discern. Learning to perceive God's voice and acting upon it is a key to living a successful Christian life. So, how does God speak to us? There are several ways. While this list is not exhaustive, it shows some of the ways God speaks to His people today:

The Bible

We have said this before, but it bears repeating. The first and foremost way we hear God speak to us is through the Bible—Holy Scripture which is His written revelation to humanity. When reading the Bible, has a verse ever just seemed to jump off the page? When that happens, it is often God communicating a particular truth to us for our particular situation. We should never underestimate the power of Scripture as an instrument of God to speak to us in a personal way. In fact, the Bible is our litmus test for any other kind of revelation we feel we are receiving. If we think we have heard God, but what we are hearing contradicts the Bible in any way, you can be sure it's not God's voice you are hearing!

God's Still, Small Voice

When God speaks to us in this way, we just know that we know something is right. We have a strong feeling to move ahead in one direction, or we find an issue in our heart has been settled, and the answer is clear to us. Some may call this intuition, or even a "sixth sense," but it is often an inaudible voice of God speaking directly into our spirits.

Other People

God can and often does speak a very direct prophetic word to us through other people. Some biblical examples of this are: King David expressing, "The Spirit of the LORD spoke through me; his word was on my tongue" (2 Samuel 23:2, NIV). Or Peter saying "But men spoke from God as they were carried along by the Holy Spirit" (2 Peter 1:21, NIV). This can happen in preaching and teaching we receive, in conversations we have, when we receive a prophetic word or a word of knowledge or wisdom, or through tongues and interpretation. No matter the method, when the Lord uses someone to speak His words to you, they hit you in a deep and profound way—like someone turning on the lights in the midst of darkness.

> Throughout the Bible, God actively disclosed Himself to humanity. ...He continues to reveal His power, His glory, His nature, His character, His will, His ways, His plans, and His strategies to His people today.

God's Creation

"For since the creation of the world God's invisible qualities – his eternal power and divine nature – have been clearly seen, being understood from what has been made, so that men are without excuse" (Romans 1:20, NIV). Have you ever felt the presence of God in a sunset, a flower, or even a raging thunderstorm? At times great beauty in nature or even in a moral truth can be a vehicle for a direct word from God. In the Bible, we see He used a rainbow as a sign of His covenant with Noah. He used dew on a fleece to help guide Gideon. He caused a fig tree that did not bear fruit to wither and die. The righteousness He makes available to us is likened throughout Scripture to white snow. If we take the time to stop and look around us, we may be surprised to find that God is speaking through His creation.

Dreams and Visions

"'We both had dreams,' they answered, 'but there is no one to interpret them.' Then Joseph said to them, 'Do not interpretations belong to God? Tell me your dreams'" (Genesis 40:8, NIV). We see many biblical examples of God speaking to His people in dreams and visions. He spoke to Joseph, Solomon, Pharaoh, many prophets and kings, and Joseph (Jesus' earthly father) by this means. Joel 2:28 says, "afterward, I will pour out my Spirit on all people. ...Your old men will dream dreams, your young men will see visions." God still speaks through dreams today. If you awake from a dream that seems unusually vivid and very real, you may want to ask the Lord if He is trying to speak something to you through that dream. We will take a much closer look at this in the next two chapters.

Experiences or Circumstances

There may be times when God speaks to you through a very specific incident. Sometimes this happens in prayer at home. Sometimes this happens when we respond to an alter call. Often this will occur when people first become saved. It may be a moment when tremendous clarity comes as a result of some incident. When God speaks to us through a specific experience, we will be able to point back to that moment in time as a benchmark for a shifting in our lives. Many times circumstances arise in our life that are perplexing. However, we need to look deep into those circumstances so we can hear clearly God's voice.

Angels

All throughout the Bible, God sent angels as His messengers to speak something to His people. This method of communication is still one He chooses to use from time to time, and one that we cannot discount. One day God may surprise you!

Audible Voice

There are times when God chooses to speak in an audible voice. He did so in young Samuel's life as well as to many others in the Bible. Genesis tells us that it was by His audible voice that God created all of heaven, earth, and every creature that has breath. Can God not use that same voice to speak to His creation?

Barriers to Revelation

Having looked at some of the ways God speaks to us, it poses the question, why don't we hear Him more often? Of course, God can choose when, where, how, and to whom He will speak. But assuming that He is attempting to communicate with us, what are some of the issues in our lives that can prevent us from gaining revelation? Here is a list of some barriers many of us have dealt with or are dealing with today:

Distractions

Have you ever found it difficult to pray; or, once you set your mind to it, you become bored and distracted? We often miss what God may be trying to say to us simply because we are unable to focus on Him. If we are having a phone conversation with someone while trying to do three other things, chances are we won't have absorbed all of the conversation. This is one of the reasons that we are exhorted by Scripture to meditate on God and His Word. If we can find a strategy to minimize our distractions, we may be amazed to hear God speaking to us. [1]

Disinformation

Often as Christians we look to our churches and our colleagues to build our theology rather than basing our doctrinal stand on what God's Word says. This is why many have come to believe that God does not speak to His children today—not because of anything the Bible has said, but because of disinformation they have received somewhere along the line. God has given us His Word and His promises, and He expects us to check our decisions and our beliefs with Scripture so that we will not get tripped up with disinformation. We are always correct to ask God to renew our minds so we conform to Him rather than to the beliefs of the world (see Romans 2:12). [2]

Disbelief

Many cannot and will not hear the voice of God in their lives because they simply do not believe. They may have come to salvation, and may even pray from time to time, but they really expect little or nothing to come of it. If we truly believed that every time we pray, God—who has control of everything in and around—not only will listen to us, but desires to converse with us, we would pray every chance we get. But often, because we don't see immediate (or what we consider to be adequate) answers to our prayers, we fall into disbelief. But we must remember that we serve an all-powerful, all-knowing God that we can trust to give us the very best in spite of what we ask for, or in spite of how we interpret His answer. If we have fallen into disbelief, our first prayer back toward God should be, "I do believe; help me overcome my unbelief!" (Mark 9:24, NIV). [3]

In our book, *Possessing Your Inheritance* (Renew), we also point out the following progression that can lead to missing God's revelation. When God does speak, we must realize that we have an enemy who immediately tries to steal from us what is rightfully ours. Satan will always attempt to thwart what God is doing. Such was the case for the Israelites. When they were coming out of their captivity in Babylon, they received a revelation from the Lord (see Jer. 29:10). The Israelites knew God's will for them was to return and rebuild the destroyed Temple of the Lord. They had clearly heard from God. But as they began working toward the restoration God had for them, the enemy resisted their efforts. Instead of fighting for what they knew they were to do, the children of Israel gave in. As the people allowed the enemy to take a foothold, three things began to happen:

1.   They fell into *discouragement*. They began to ask why God was calling them to rebuild the Temple in the first place.

2.   Then they fell into *disillusionment*. Things weren't going well, so they began to wonder if God had really told them to build at all.

3.   Finally they fell into *disinterest*. As the situation progressed, they decided they would build their own houses and leave His in disrepair. They stopped caring.

This progression of events is often a pattern for what can happen in our own lives if we do not guard what the Lord has told us and seriously pursue His will. It takes an act of our own will to choose God's plan for possessing our inheritance.[4]

Processing Revelation

God had a purpose in having the Israelites rebuild His temple. It was not because God was being selfish. Rebuilding had a direct effect on restoring to the Israelites what had been lost through their captivity in Babylon. It was important for their future. When God brings revelation into our lives, it is not an end in itself, but is part of a process intended to move us toward our potential and our destiny. In this book, we have looked at the value of prophecy in our lives. Prophecy, as well as the majority of revelation we receive, moves us through the following process:

1. God tells us about Himself. Oftentimes, He will use the Bible as His means of communicating with us about who He is. Even when He uses other methods, they will always align with what the Bible has to say. Therefore, it is imperative that we become as familiar as we can with the Word of God.

2. God tells us what He has planned.

3. God then tells us that we are a part of the plan.

Not everyone is open to receiving what God has to say. This is because whenever revelation comes from God, it directly confronts us. When we are confronted with truth from God, we must deal with it on some level. Revelation from God requires a response from us. While it is true that God is sovereign, we must respond to His sovereignty in order for His will to be done.

God's revelation comes to us, not as information for our brains to process, but as a mandate for our faith to arise and as a guide to conduct our lives. Without faith it is impossible to please God. Equally true, however, is that faith without actions is dead. Revelation challenges us on both levels. Once we gain revelation, we are obligated to that revelation. We become accountable for what God has revealed to us. In order to reach our destiny, we must receive revelation from God, and then act accordingly. Of course, sometimes the most appropriate reaction is to wait on God with expectancy, but the principle remains the same. It is when we do not act upon the revelation we receive that windows of opportunity can close, sometimes forever.

Walking in revelation and reaching our destiny in God can be summed up very simply: In every circumstance we find ourselves, we must find God's sovereign plan within that circumstance and be faithful to walk in His will.

Notes
1 Taken from Marilyn Willett Heavilin, *I'm Listening, Lord* (Nashville, Tenn.: Thomas Nelson Publishers, 1993), pp. 33-37.
2 Ibid., pp. 49-51.
3 Ibid., pp. 54-57.
4 Chuck D. Pierce and Rebecca Wagner Sytsema, *Possessing Your Inheritance* (Ventura, Calif.: Renew, 1999), pp. 100-101.

CHAPTER FIVE

Hearing God Through Dreams and Visions

Then He said, "Hear now My words: if there is a prophet among you, I, the LORD, make Myself known to him in a vision; I speak to him in a dream" (Num. 12:6).

We concluded the last chapter by saying that in every circumstance we find ourselves, we must find God's sovereign plan within that circumstance and be faithful to walk in His will. One of the primary ways that God has always used to communicate with His people is through dreams and visions, yet they are often misunderstood, dismissed, or ignored. Dreams particularly can seem foolish or strange. But as Ira Milligan points out, "Paul said that God chose the foolish things of the world to confound the wise (see 1 Cor. 1:27). Although many dreams are foolish or senseless to the world, they are precious to those who understand 'the hidden wisdom' from above (1 Cor. 2:7)." [1]

Fiona Starr and Jonny Zucker point out, "The Old Testament is laden with dream scenes and interpretations. One of the best known is the story of Jacob's son, Joseph. Joseph was said to hold the power of forecasting through his dreams. Joseph's dream analyses were often the cause of much sibling rivalry, not only because of the unique power that Joseph possessed, but also because of the content of the dreams. In many of his dreams Joseph dreamt of himself as the superior brother. The others grew angry with Joseph's seeming arrogance and tried to exile him while convincing Jacob that his favorite son was dead. Joseph's power, however, helped him find his way out of a dangerous situation when he was able to help Pharaoh of Egypt interpret his own dreams.

"Jacob's ladder is another well-known biblical dream story. Some say that the dream of the ladder resting on earth but leading up to the heavens is a symbol for higher communication between God and humans on earth." [2]

In the Bible there are over 50 references for messages being sent by God through dreams and visions to both the righteous and the unrighteous alike. The Lord used dreams and visions to guide, to warn, to direct, to help, and to communicate His heart. God has not stopped communicating to humanity by these means. In fact, God often uses dreams and visions to reach unsaved individuals with the Gospel, particularly in closed parts of the world. In Global Harvest Ministries, where I serve as Vice President, we recently reported one such story:

"An Iranian living near Kassel told a Christian worker of a dream he recently had: 'I was standing on the roof of my house when a bright light like a spotlight shone on me. This light then moved down to illuminate a stream, which seemed to be made of light. I don't know what it means. I have consulted books and visited dream interpreters, but I can find no answer.' 'Only God can interpret dreams,' the Christian visitor told him, telling him that Jesus is the light of the world. 'The light shining on you means that Jesus is calling you, and the stream could be an indication that you should be baptized.' The Iranian was convinced, and agreed to follow Jesus and be baptized." [3]

We have scores of similar testimonies of dreams and visions being used by God to draw individuals, families, and entire communities to Himself. Similarly, the Lord uses this method of revelation in the lives of most, if not all, believers.

What is a Dream?

A dream is a release of revelation (whether natural or spiritual) that comes at a time when your body is at peace and you are settled. Sometimes this is the only way God can communicate with us because our soul is quiet enough for the Lord to speak deeply into our spirit. A dream is like a snapshot of something you are able to relate to in picture form. Ecclesiastes 5:3 tells us that a dream comes when there are many cares. They can either be a subconscious response to the circumstances of our lives, or the Holy Spirit communicating to us. As Jane Hamon states in her book, *Dreams and Visions*, "Dreams are formed in the subconscious mind of a man or woman based on images and symbols which are unique to the individual, depending on his or her background, experience and current life circumstances. Dreams can communicate to us truth about ourselves—or others— which our conscious mind may have failed to acknowledge.

"Dreams can originate strictly within the natural mind or can be given as messages from God's Spirit and received within the mind of man. ...If we compare the communication of the Spirit of the Lord through dreams to other methods of divine communication mentioned in Scripture—prophecy, a word of knowledge, etc.—the primary difference is that dreams are given first to our subconscious minds before being perceived by our conscious minds." [4]

In the ancient eastern world dreams were treated as reality. Dreams were considered to be the world of the divine or the demonic. They often revealed the future. Dreams could be filled with revelation that would cause the dreamer to make the right decision for his or her future.

> All dreams have some level of significance in our lives, and it is important to invite the Lord into the process of determining what the level of significance of each dream may be.

Israel was forbidden to use many of the same type of divining practices as Egypt and other neighboring countries and peoples. However, God would visit them in the night to communicate His will and way to them. This continued throughout the Bible. In the first two chapters of the New Testament alone, God gives direction through prophetic dreams five times.

We as Christians can also receive revelation from dreams that are inspired by the Holy Spirit. For instance, I once had a dream when I was in prayer for a trip to Israel. My good friend and colleague, Bobbye Byerly and I were going to be leading prayer for a meeting that would reconcile Arab Christian leaders and Messianic leaders. Peter Wagner was going to be facilitating this meeting. There was quite a bit of warfare surrounding this meeting. I became very troubled while praying and called Bobbye to tell her that we should pray and fast for three days before going. Bobbye was having the same burden and agreed immediately.

On the second day of the fast I fell asleep and dreamed that Barbara Wentroble, a well known prophet, asked me, "So, you are going to Israel. There are two ways. Which way are you taking?" I told her the way we were going. In the dream it was as if I was showing her a map and we were wandering through the Arab desert to get to Israel. She then said, "You may go that way, but if you do, you will experience much warfare. There is a better way for you to take." I said, "Oh, what is that way?" She replied, "Go straight to Israel and meet with the leadership you know. Then, have your meeting with everyone else." I woke up and knew that God had revealed to me the direction for Peter Wagner as he proceeded in pulling together this meeting. I encouraged him to first have a meeting with the leaders of Israel that we knew. Then we could have the overall meeting and reconciliation time. This proved to be direct revelation from God and had a significant impact on the overall outcome of our mission.

What is a Vision?

The easiest way to describe a vision is as if you are having a dream, but you are awake. To those experiencing a vision, it will often seem as if they have entered into a different reality because they are seeing with their spiritual eyes images of items and events that are not physically there. Others in the room may not see what is going on. That is because what is being perceived by the one or ones having the vision is a spiritual event.

The borderline between vision and dream is sometimes difficult, if not impossible, to determine. The circumstances in which
the revelatory visions came to the seers of the Bible are varied.
They came in waking hours (Dn. 10:7; Acts 9:7); by day (Acts
10:3) or by night (Gn. 46:2). But the visions had close connections
with the dream-state (Nu. 12:6; Jb. 4:13).

In the Old Testament, the recipients of revelatory visions were
the prophets, 'writing' (Is. 1:1; Ob. 1; Na. 1:1) and 'non-writing' (2
Sa. 7:17; 1 Ki. 22:17-19; 2 Ch. 9:29). But the outstanding examples were Ezekiel and Daniel. Luke, in the New Testament,
manifests the greatest interest in visions. He reports the visions of
Zechariah (Lk. 1:22), Ananias (Acts 9:10), Cornelius (10:3), Peter
(10:10ff.), and Paul (18:9). We find Paul treating visions with
much reserve (2 Cor. 12:1ff.). The Book of Revelation is the ultimate vision. [5]

In *The Future War of the Church*, Rebecca and I share an in-
depth vision that the Lord gave me on December 31, 1985. Even
though I dream often, I have only had five visions that were significant enough for me to record. This detailed vision gave direction for the changes in the Church of the future. It also warned of
militant Islam and lawless acts coming against the Church. You
can read the details of this in Chapter One of *The Future War of the
Church*. [6]

My Pastor is Robert Heidler. His wife, Linda, is a wonderful,
prophetic prayer leader and minister. She had the following vision, which I love:

"In March of 1997, we were in a Sunday morning church
service. I began to have a vision. In this vision I knew that
the Lord was coming to visit my house. I had cleaned

everything cleaner than ever before. My carpets were cleaned, my curtains were washed and ironed, and everything was dusted and polished. I had fresh flowers on the table. I could not think of anything else that could be done to make my house ready for the Lord to come. It was the best it could possibly be.

All at once the Lord was standing in my house. He had not come to the door, He just appeared. I did not know what to say or do. He looked around then pointed to one wall of my living room and said, 'That whole wall has to go.' I was in shock. That wall was the one between my living room and garage. My washer and dryer were on the other side of that wall. I wanted to protest, but as the Lord spoke the words, the wall shattered. Sheet rock, two-by-fours and wires were sticking out and the room was covered in plaster dust.

Before I could recover from that, the Lord pointed to a room off the back of my house. In reality I did not have a room like this, only in the vision. This room had all kinds of awards, pictures, trophies, medals, etc. It also had family heirlooms. The Lord pointed to that room and said, 'That whole room has to go.' Immediately I thought of getting all my treasures out, but the Lord said, 'And don't try to get anything out either.' As I looked, a huge crane appeared in my back yard and a wrecking ball swung across and demolished the room.

My house was a wreck, I was in shock and did not know what to do. This was not what I had anticipated, but it was very clearly what the Lord knew needed to happen in my house."

This vision speaks for itself. The Lord is saying, "Even though you've got everything in order, get ready for the changes I am bringing!"

What is a Night Vision?

There are several references in the Scripture to "night visions." A night vision occurs when we are not sure if we are asleep or awake, and it tends to be right to the point.

In Acts 16:9-10 we read, "And a vision appeared to Paul in the night. A man of Macedonia stood and pleaded with him, saying, 'Come over to Macedonia and help us.' Now after he had seen the vision, immediately we sought to go to Macedonia, concluding that the Lord had called us to preach the gospel to them."

Ira Milligan offers this insight: "There is a difference between a dream and a night vision. A night vision requires little or no interpretation. In addition to the actual vision seen, a night vision usually has a voice speaking that gives the primary meaning of the vision. In contrast, a dream seldom lends itself to self-interpretation." [7]

Discernment is Key!

Whether we are talking about dreams, visions, or night visions, we need to recognize that not all revelation coming by these means is necessarily inspired by God. There are three different categories of dreams and visions, each of which can be traced to different sources:

1. Spiritual dreams and vision, which are inspired by God's Spirit.
2. Natural, or soulful dreams and visions, which are produced by the natural processes of a person's mind, will, and emotions.
3. False or occultic dreams and visions. [8]

It is important for us to exercise discernment in determining the source of dreams and visions. Without this, we can be basing our life decisions on soulish desires, or the enemy could gain a ready inroad to thwart us in our destiny. Adapted from Jane Hamon's book, here is a list of questions to ask as you determine what is behind a dream or vision:

1.   Is the message of the dream or vision consistent with the teachings, character, and nature of Jesus? All revelation from spiritual dreams and visions will lead us into a closer, more committed relationship with God.

2.   Does the message of the dream or vision lead to righteousness? If the message of the dream is more self-serving or speaks to soulish desires, it may not be a spiritual dream.

3.   Is the message of the dream or vision consistent with doctrine, teaching, and principles from the Word of God? All spiritual dreams or visions will support and emphasize biblical truths.

4.   Do you feel a stirring of your spirit or emotions upon awaking? In the book of Daniel we see that the king had a dream which greatly disturbed him. When you feel impacted by a dream, it could be an indication that God is speaking to you.

5.   Does the dream or vision cause you to search your soul, or have pressing questions been answered within the context of the dream?

6.   Is the dream recurring or similar to others you've had? While this alone is not an indicator of a spiritual dream, in the context of the other questions posed here, it could offer a clue that the Lord is trying to get your attention repeatedly. [9]

Always Talk to God About Your Dreams

If, after reading these questions and applying your God-given discernment, you determine that your dream is more of a natural or soulful origin, or perhaps it is more demonic in nature, do not be discouraged. No matter what the origin of a dream we have had, we can and should always talk to the Lord about what we have dreamed. We should not ignore what a dream may reveal about our emotions, and can always ask God to clarify puzzling or disturbing dreams so He can bring His comfort and healing to our mind, will, and emotions.

If we discern that a dream is demonic in nature, it might be an indication of how the enemy is working to thwart us, or could be a call to a new level of spiritual warfare. All dreams have some level of significance in our lives, and it is important to invite the Lord into the process of determining what the level of significance of each dream may be.

Lean Not on Your Own Understanding

Many of us have been in very difficult places. There was a particular time in my wife, Pam's, and my own life, where we had almost insurmountable issues all around us. During the night Pam had a dream. In the dream she was on a path. This path was leading through a wooded area. Even so, she could see the sun. As long as she would keep her eyes on the sun, she could keep moving forward. Even though the light got brighter and brighter, when she got close to the end of the path, there was a huge boulder. The boulder extended itself out into the forest as well as completely blocking the path. She said that during the dream she began to *think*, "How can I get past this? I must get out to the other side." She then heard a voice say, "Don't try and go around this blockade. Don't try and go over it. Don't try and go through it. Speak to it and tell it to move."

When she got up that morning, she said, "We are going to speak to the issues that are coming against us." We began to take each one and speak and make prophetic declaration to it, and we watched changes begin to take place.

Proverbs 3:5-6 says, "Trust in the LORD with all your heart, And lean not on your own understanding; in all your ways acknowledge

Him, and He shall direct your paths." Seek God. Listen carefully. Let Him speak to you. Lean not on your own understanding, but let Him give you the way through your circumstance.

Now let's take an in-depth look at interpreting dreams and visions.

Notes

[1] Ira Milligan, *Understanding the Dreams You Dream* (Shippensburg, PA: Treasure House, 1997), p. 3.

[2] Fiona Starr and Jonny Zucker: *Dream Themes: A Guide to Understanding Your Dreams* (China: Barnes & Noble Books, 2001), p. 10.

[3] "Praying Around the World," *The Prayer Track News* (Vol. 8, No. 2, Apr - Jun, 1999), p. 8.

[4] Jane Hamon, *Dreams and Visions* (Ventura, CA: Regal Books, 2000), pp. 22-24.

[5] Bibliography. J. M. Lower, 'Vision', *ZPEB*, 5, p. 889; R. Schnackenburg, 'Vision of God', *EBT*, 3, pp. 947-952; K. Dahn, *NIDNTT* 3, pp. 511-518.

[6] Chuck D. Pierce and Rebecca Wagner Sytsema, *The Future War of the Church* (Ventura CA: Renew Books, 2001), pp. 28-35.

[7] Milligan, pp. 9-10.

[8] Hamon, p. 37.

[9] Ibid., pp. 60-63.

CHAPTER SIX

Interpreting Dreams and Visions

"For God may speak in one way, or in another, yet man does not perceive it. In a dream, in a vision of the night, when deep sleep falls upon men, while slumbering on their beds, Then He opens the ears of men, and seals their instruction" (Job 33:14-16).

Whether or not we are aware of it, God often reveals instructions to us through dreams. We may not even remember the dream, but often we will awaken with a new sense of clarity because God has spoken to us in the night. Because God will often seal our instructions through dreams, we need to know how to properly interpret them.

In the Bible, prophecy and dreams were to be tested in the same way and, according to Numbers 12:6, we find that prophecy and dreams are treated equally. Saul complained that God would not speak to him or answer him "by dreams, by urim or by prophets" (1 Sam. 28:6). By this we can infer that these were normal ways that people would hear from God. There are three types of dreams that we find in the Bible:

1. **A simple message dream.** Joseph in Matthew 1-2 understood the dreams concerning Mary and Herod. There was really no need for interpretation. These dreams were direct, to the point, and interpreted themselves.

2. **The simple symbolic dream.** Dreams can be filled with symbols. Oftentimes the symbolism is clear enough that the dreamer and others can understand it without any complicated interpretation. For instance, when Joseph had his dream in Genesis 37, he fully understood it, as did his brothers, to the point that they wanted to kill him, even though it had symbols of the sun, moon and stars.

3. **The complex symbolic dream.** This third type of dream needs interpretative skill from someone who has unusual ability in the gift of interpretation or someone who knows how to seek God to find revelation. We find this in the life of Joseph in prison as well, when he interprets Pharaoh's dream. In Daniel 2 and 4, we find good examples of this type of dream. In Daniel 8, we see a dream where Daniel actually had to seek divine interpretation.

Understanding symbols is important not only to interpret our own dreams, but to give some direction to those who come to us. Just as we mentioned in the last chapter, God speaks to unbelievers through dreams. I would prophetically say that this is only going to increase in days ahead, and God will need believers who know how to discern and interpret in order to lead many to Christ. It is our job as ambassadors for Christ to be carriers and interpreters of God's revelation in this age.

Daniel's Model of Interpretation

As we think about the process of dream and/or vision interpretation, the book of Daniel gives us a good pattern to follow. This is the story of King Nebuchadnezzar's dreams and the process through which Daniel interpreted them:

1. Daniel determined the source of the dreams and knew they were a message from God. This is the first step, which we have already discussed.

2. Daniel asked for time to interpret the dream (2:16). First Corinthians 2:6 says, "We do, however, speak a message of wisdom among the mature, but not the wisdom of this age or of the rulers of this age, who are coming to nothing." In other words, we have wisdom that no one else has access to—wisdom that comes from the Lord. We often need time to seek the Lord for His interpretation, as well as wisdom from those God has placed in our lives.

3. Daniel gathered intercession by urging His friends to seek the Lord (2:18). There are times when we need to soak the dream or vision in prayer and ask those around us to intercede on our behalf until clear interpretation of the vision comes from God.

4. Daniel gained revelation from the Lord (2:19). As we pursue an interpretation, there are certain questions that are helpful in gaining revelation over the dream or vision. They include:

- Who does the dream refer to?
- What is it really about?
- What is the setting or settings?
- What is the symbolism in the dream (more about this a little further down)?
- What are the current circumstances and history of the one who received the dream or vision?
- When we have a handle on the interpretation, we need to ask what is God's timing in fulfilling the dream or vision?
- Based on this dream, what responsibility does the one who received the dream or vision have?

5.   Daniel worshiped God (2:20-23). It is so important to give God glory and worship Him for both the dream or vision, and the interpretation. When we miss this we miss the next step of revelation in our lives.

6.   Daniel explained the dream (2:36-45). When we are interpreting a dream for someone else, we need to be sensitive as to how the Lord would have us explain the interpretation.

Modern Day Dreams and Interpretations

When I was coming into the things of the Lord and the Spirit, the Lord placed a wonderful mentor in my life. LaCelia Henderson was a teacher in the public schools and a wonderful Bible teacher as well. Most importantly, she understood this spiritual realm that I was just learning to maneuver in. I want to encourage each of you reading this book to find someone who can help you as you move into receiving supernatural revelation. She had a dream that really has "stuck" with me through the years.

In the dream I had gone with friends (Charles and Charlene) to a cabin they had in the woods. We were dressed for bed when someone knocked at the door. Charlene started to answer the door and I waited in the bedroom. I said I would hide back there while she answered the door. If it was a friend I would come out and if not I would jump out the window and run for help. When she opened the door these men came in who were dressed in army fatigues. They came in like the Gestapo and took the place by storm (captured it). In the meantime I had jumped out of the window in my nightgown. When they saw the open window they knew that I had escaped. Some of them ran outside and got in a vehicle (like a jeep) to look for me. It was very, very dark; I was alone and vulnerable (in my nightgown). Their eyes were very piercing as they scanned to and fro trying to spot me. When they were not looking my way I would run from tree to tree. It was all very intense and I had very little time to get behind the next tree before they looked back my way each time. Finally, I came to a clearing and I saw some houses. But, I knew that I had to choose the house I ran to very carefully. It had to be someone who knew me and trusted me. I knew that once I stepped out into the clearing that I would be spotted. I also knew that when I ran to a house to use the telephone to call for help I would not have time to explain the situation to get permission to use the telephone. If I took time to explain I would be caught and stopped by the enemy. Once I got to the house I had to be able to run straight to the phone to make the call for help.

When I asked her to write this dream, she commented to me, "After all these years (at this time it has been 15), I can still remember every detail of this dream vividly." This dream was a warning! Not only did it warn of the need to know your relationships in the future, it explained Christians would go into a new dimension of persecution. This was a dream that activated discernment and wisdom. A Scripture reference that would be very appropriate for this dream would be 1 Samuel 18:14: "And David behaved wisely in all his ways, and the Lord was with him. Therefore, when Saul saw he behaved wisely, he was afraid of him." First Samuel 20:3 says, "But truly as the Lord lives and as your soul lives there is but a step between me and death." This dream revealed a changing government status and from a spiritual stand-point showed that the "Saul government" of the Church would persecute those that were moving into a new wineskin.

In *The Future War of the Church,* Rebecca and I shared this when we were listing the guidelines that will assist us in maintaining our spiritual focus and know the times we are living in:

"We must know how to get in touch with each other immediately. Maintaining our connections and relationships with each other is another key to securing our future. God sovereignly connects and aligns us with one another, so we can function effectively. Know with whom God has connected you and how to let them know what God is saying to you. This will keep God's warning system in proper order. One way that we remain connected is through frequent gatherings. In Genesis 49, we read that Jacob called his sons together and revealed their futures to them. The Lord is using prophetic gatherings today in much the same way. As we come together corporately, God will speak to us and reveal things we may not see on an individual basis. Another method God is raising up to maintain connections is through organizations like the World Prayer Center in Colorado Springs. The World Prayer Center uses state-of-the-art communications technology to both gather and disseminate information to praying people throughout the world on urgent matters that require immediate, fervent prayer. This is one way God is connecting the Body of Christ in order to secure the future harvest." [1]

Kristine Herman, who works for Wagner Leadership Institute, had the following interesting dream:

In my dream, I was seated in a large room with tables and people were eating and fellowshipping. I was seated and a man in a short-sleeved white sweater came up to me and told me that he thought the Lord wanted him to give me some money so he gave me some cash. He ended up coming back several times and giving me more money. I didn't look to see how much he had given me. I got up from my chair and was walking away, looking in my wallet to see how much money he had given me. I found two one hundred dollar bills along with some smaller bills totaling $250 to $300. I also found a blank check that he had signed. His name (Larry) and his wife's names were at the upper left corner of the check. I also had a credit card form with his credit card information on it and this, too, was signed by Larry.

Kristine was able to interpret this dream immediately. She says, "My understanding while I was looking at the check and the credit card form was that I could purchase whatever I desired and there was no limit to the amount I could spend. I could pay off my mortgage with his personal check and that would be just fine." I would think God would give a dream like this to someone when they were in a difficult place financially or else they are moving forward into an expanded vision and need to know that God is going to provide for them.

Interpreting Symbolism

In most dreams recorded in the Bible, God used a tremendous amount of symbolism to convey His message. Jesus often used parables when making His points. This has not changed through the years. The vast majority of dreams and visions are laden with symbolic imagery. It is often helpful, therefore, to have a basic understanding of symbolism and to have reference books on hand with helpful, biblically-based lists of symbols and types.[2] We have included an appendix in this book that includes some basic symbols.

Snails and Turtles

I once had a dream about a friend in McAllen, Texas. In the dream, my friend was walking along a path that was filled with snails. If the man did not stomp on the snails, they would turn into snakes that hissed and bit. Then there were many turtles, and if my friend would keep in line with the turtles, they would lead him safely to his destination.

As God showed me the interpretation, the snails represented business associates that were linked with legal entities who had the ability to turn and bite. Through the turtles, God was saying that he needed to slow things down in order to prosper. As I shared this with my friend, he was amazed. At that time, he was involved in three separate law suits, and there were many "snails" in his life. The dream gave him wisdom as to how to proceed with these associates. Also, because he heeded the warning of the turtles and slowed things down, he did prosper and was ultimately successful in all his law suits and in his business ventures.

Symbols Are Flexible

Ira Milligan adds the following thoughts on interpreting symbols: "Almost all symbols can have both positive (good) and negative (bad) meanings. ...The most important thing to remember about interpreting symbols is, *never be narrow-minded*. Symbols, like words, are very flexible. When one knows the context of a dream and the circumstances of the dreamer's life, one can properly assign the right meanings. Without this knowledge one can only guess.

"For instance, it is possible for an ant in a dream to mean several different things ...[these include] industrious; wise; diligent; prepared for the future; nuisance; stinging or angry words. When one dreams of ants at a picnic, the context would obviously lean toward 'nuisance' as the meaning of the symbol, even though it is their industrious nature that makes them such a nuisance! To dream of ants gathering food would relate directly to the key word definition of industrious, diligent preparation for the future. Likewise, dreaming of being bit or stung by ants would fit the 'stinging or angry words' definition.

> Chances are that whether or not you have been aware of it, you have received messages from God in your dreams.

"Sometimes a symbol has a meaning to one person that would not fit another. ...When trying to decipher a symbol, the first question we should ask is, 'What does this symbol mean to [*the dreamer*]?'" [3]

A Complex Dream

In the spring of 1996, Linda Heidler had this dream while I was in Israel:

In the dream I was with a large group of people out in a desert place. There was a lot of sand blowing which would get into your eyes. I remember that my hair kept blowing into my face. We were all watching a woman who was seated at a large machine. She was sitting on a high stool behind the machine. The machine had lots of levers, pulleys, gears, buttons, pedals, etc. One by one the people from the crowd would stand in front of the machine and the woman would begin to talk to them. As she talked to them she would start working the pedals and pulling the levers. She was moving constantly as she spoke to them. She would tell them things they needed to let go of and things they needed to increase in. As she spoke and worked the machine, the people all turned into triangles. When she was finished, she would put the person into a clear plastic container like tupperware and seal them. When she had finished with two people she would put them together and they would form a Star of David, then they would go off together as happy as could be.

As we watched we would look at the person she was working on and would say, "There is no way she can make them into a triangle." But one after another they would all form into triangles. When we saw who she was going to pair up to form the Star of David we would also say, "There is no way those two will ever match up." But when she finished they were perfectly matched and very happy.

When it was my turn to stand in front of the machine and she began to talk to me and operate the machine, it was just wonderful! Everything she said made so much sense. It was so wise and freeing and practical. I loved it! When she finished, I was a triangle. She then put me in the tupperware and sealed me. I could not feel anything different, but noticed that the sand was not blowing in my eyes anymore and my hair was not blowing in my face. I do not remember who I was matched up with to form the Star of David, but I felt complete.

This is a great example of a complex symbolic dream. First of all, this had relevance in Linda's life. Second of all, it applied to the trip that I was on in Israel. I have explained this earlier concerning my dream of Israel that Barbara Wentroble was in. And third, it had a great relevance concerning covenant alignment. To fully interpret the dream, I used Scripture as well as an understanding of symbols. I used several Scriptures to help in the interpretation of this dream along with word of wisdom:

1. **Workmanship.** Ephesians 2:10: "For we are His workmanship, created in Christ Jesus for good works, which God prepared beforehand that we should walk in them."

2. **Sealed.** Second Corinthians 1:22: "who also has sealed us and given us the Spirit in our hearts as a guarantee." Ephesians 4:30: "And do not grieve the Holy Spirit of God, by whom you were sealed for the day of redemption."

3. **Joined.** First Corinthians 1:10: "Now I plead with you, brethren, by the name of our Lord Jesus Christ, that you all speak the same thing, and that there be no divisions among you, but that you be perfectly joined together in the same mind and in the same judgment." First Corinthians 6:17: "But he who is joined to the Lord is one spirit with Him." Ephesians 4:16: "from whom the whole body, joined and knit together by what every joint supplies, according to the effective working by which every part does its share, causes growth of the body for the edifying of itself in love."

4. **Transformed.** Romans 12:1-2: "I beseech you therefore, brethren, by the mercies of God, that you present your bodies a living sacrifice, holy, acceptable to God, which is your reasonable service. And do not be conformed to this world, but be transformed by the renewing of your mind, that you may prove what is that good and acceptable and perfect will of God."

It would take quite a bit of space to write the full interpretation of this dream. But I think when you read the dream along with these Scriptures you will find application to your life as well.

Symbolic Language

When we sleep we are set aside from the contact of the culture and world around us. Therefore, if we dream we can sometimes seem less civilized than our surroundings but we can also seem wiser in our dreams than when we are awake. There is a world of pictures, images and silence that we really do not perceive in fullness many times when we are awake.

In his book, *Dreams*, Rabbi Shmuel Boteach states, "Symbolic language is a language in which inner experiences, feelings, and thoughts are expressed as if they were sensory experience or events in the real world. It is a language which has a different logic from the one we use while awake. By this logic, it is not time and space which are the ruling categories, as they are in the real world. Rather, symbolic language is governed by categories of intensity and association. It is a language with its own grammar and syntax, as it were, and a language one must understand if one is to comprehend the meaning of Midrashim, myths, and dreams. Symbolic language is the one universal language the human race has constantly developed. Yet it has been forgotten by modern man. Although he may still write his dreams with it, he is at a loss to decipher it when he awakens." [4]

Replacing Symbols with Key Words

Once we have an idea of what the symbols represent, we can follow Daniel's example of interpreting the king's dream. He simply replaced the symbols with the key words or patterns that they represented in order to decipher the message in the dream. So, using the dream I had of my friend in McAllen, Texas, the simple interpretation would be that he was moving along in business (represented by the path), and that certain business associates surrounding him (represented by the snails) would turn and bite him (represented by the snakes) if he did not deal with them appropriately (represented by the stomping). Then the dream shifted to reveal that he would have to get in step with God's timing, which was slower than he was going (represented by following in line with the turtles) in order to prosper (represented by the safe destination).

When interpreting symbols for others, it is important to remember that we should not impose our interpretation of symbols if it is not bearing witness with the dreamer.

Your Sons and Your Daughters Shall Prophesy...

My children have many dreams. Most of them have a real prophetic bent to them. They have always been taught to listen carefully for the voice of God in their dreams. Pam and I try to let them share their dreams, good or bad, and then discuss various spiritual insights with them. Daniel, one of our older sons, had a dream a few years ago of watching the Chinese army muster to invade our nation. We had many discussions about this. Our daughter, Rebekah, had the following dream when she was 16:

My friend Randi and I were driving in the Expedition (our family vehicle). Randi was actually driving, and I was in the front passenger seat. I looked out the window and saw debris all around us. We were in a suburban area that had been blown up. I was probably in my early 20s (three or four years older than when I had the dream). I saw children playing in the debris. I also saw a family with a father and three boys. The boys were likely 17, 13, and 10 years old. They all looked alike. The four of them were holding hands as they walked through the debris. As they walked up to the car Randi introduced me. The father recognized me and said, "Its nice to meet you. My wife used to be a big fan of yours." I was perplexed at why he used the past tense in referring to his wife. I next shook hands with the oldest son, and felt like I knew him. Then we said we'd see them at the Love Feast at the church, and drove off.

When we arrived at the church, the church itself was completely intact, but everything around it was blown up. I saw my friend, Micah, in the welcome center. As I walked over to see him, I came past the area where brochures are displayed. Underneath the announcement center at the church was a family photograph. It had matting and three photos of the same family that I had just seen on the drive to church. In the first picture, they were happy and content. There was a woman in the picture who was smiling. The second picture was just of the father and boys. They looked very different. The third picture was just of oldest son. In the photo, it appeared as if he had his hands pushing away the camera. I did not understand why this picture was included. As I visited with another friend at church, I kept thinking that I needed to help my friend, Heather, but didn't know where she was. I seemed to get distracted in conversation, but my overriding thought was that I needed to help Heather.

At this point, the whole dream repeated itself a second time. The dream then repeated itself a third time. However, this time the atmosphere had changed for the worse.

At the church I went into the nursery to help Heather. The nursery was completely destroyed. In this portion of the dream I was 10 years older, and was a doctor. I turned to a lady and told her that her child would be fine. Heather was at the opposite door in the nursery. She had a baby who I knew would be fine. Upon leaving the nursery I was much younger again. Things had not been destroyed and things looked as they presently are today. I met someone in the hall who shared they were happy for me. I noticed Mom was in the church entrance. I overheard her say there was a new family coming to the church who's mother was really sick. At this point, that family entered the building and I realized it was the family at the beginning of my dream. The mother had cancer and was dying. When I saw and shook the oldest boy's hand, I asked him if we met before. He said, "No." That is where the dream ended.

This is a very interesting dream with great spiritual significance. The dream is a three-tiered dream. The dream reveals three stages of Rebekah's life, and three stages of the family's life. The dream also reveals three stages of destruction resulting in future restoration. The dream reveals three stages of the Church in days ahead. And notice the dream repeated itself three times. Generally if a dream is repeated, it becomes a very sure and necessary revelation for the future. I could take this dream and begin to prophesy tremendously to us. I would say this, "Fear not the devastation ahead, for God has a restorative plan. He will be bringing in many who are sick and afflicted. He will be restoring families. If we will follow Him and feast with Him we will always be successful in the destiny of our life."

How Do We Prepare to Receive Dreams From God?

Chances are that whether or not you have been aware of it, you have received messages from God in your dreams. Now that you have a bit more understanding, here is a list of practical things you can do to prepare yourself for these occurrences in the future:

1. Keep an open mind. Don't be frightened about receiving God-inspired dreams.

2. Make sure your bedroom is in peace and conducive to hearing the Spirit of God. If you have ungodly objects, such as gargoyle statues or Ouija Boards in your bedroom, or anywhere in your home for that matter, the Spirit of God will not be able to flow as freely because you have an open door to demonic activity. Do all you can to invite the Holy Spirit into your bedroom. [5]

3. Ask what your sleep habits are like. Do you have sleep deprivation? Is your sleep often interrupted? Often the enemy will attempt to keep you from being refreshed so it is difficult to perceive what God is saying. Try to get your sleep patterns in good order so your sleep is refreshing and rejuvenating.

4. Pray before you go to sleep and ask the Lord to speak to you and expect to receive spiritual dreams.

5. Have a pen and notebook near your bed to write impressions down. If it is easier, keep a tape recorder nearby. Record every detail you can remember. If you can remember it, there may be a good reason. Record the setting, the progression, the symbols, colors, people—everything you can remember. Also, if your dream changes scenes, continue to record it as one dream because, even though it may have different scenes, it is probably all one message. It is also a good idea to keep a dream diary so you have a record to refer to in days ahead. Often the Lord will use a series

of dreams to convey a message. It is possible to miss the full impact of what God is saying without this kind of record.

6. Ask the Lord to help you remember your dreams. Dreams are fleeting. Job 20:8 says, "He will fly away like a dream, and not be found; yes, he will be chased away like a vision of the night." There is often a short span of time when that portion of our memory is working. Also, we have not trained ourselves to remember dreams because few of us have understood their true significance. Of course there will be times when we still cannot remember our dreams, but the Lord can help us with our recall.

7. Because we generally do have a short window of time upon awakening that our dreams will be more vivid, give yourself time when you awaken so you can record your dreams and can meditate before the Lord. I always give myself about half an hour between the time I awaken and the time I get out of bed to meditate on what the Lord may have been speaking to me in the night. This is a good time to ask God to begin giving you an interpretation of what you dreamed.

8. As we have stated throughout this book, all revelation from God requires some response from us. Be sure that you are responding to the revelation God gives you through your dreams in the same way you would to a prophetic word or to other Holy Spirit-inspired revelation in your life.

Notes
[1] Chuck D. Pierce and Rebecca Wagner Sytsema, *The Future War of the Church* (Ventura, CA: Renew Books, 2001), pp. 22-23.
[2] Some excellent resources for interpreting symbols are listed in the Recommended Reading appendix beginning on page 115.
[3] Ira Milligan, *Understanding the Dreams You Dream* (Shippensburg, PA: Treasure House, 1997), pp. 31-33.

[4] Rabbi Shmuel Boteach, *Dreams* (Brooklyn NY: bp, 1991), p. 17.

[5] For further insight into spiritual housecleaning, we highly recommend *Ridding Your Home of Spiritual Darkness* by Chuck D. Pierce and Rebecca Wagner Sytsema.

CHAPTER SEVEN

God is Ready to Perform His Word!

"You will be a joy to all generations, for I will make you so.
...You will know at last that I, the LORD, am your Savior and
Redeemer, the Mighty One of Israel. ...Salvation will surround you
like city walls, and praise will be on the lips of all who enter there.
...All your people will be righteous.
...The tiniest group will become a mighty nation. I, the LORD, will
bring it all to pass at the right time."
(Isaiah 60:15-22)

When we hear God's voice, we should allow our expectations in Him to arise! In *The Best Is Yet Ahead* (Wagner Publications), Rebecca and I explain that future and expectation are synonymous. Our future is linked with an expectation of God moving. This is a time for the Church to have its expectation level renewed and raised to another level. Isaiah 59 and 60 are a wonderful prayer guide to see this happen in your life. Hope must transcend and move into faith. Faith produces overcoming. Overcoming leads to a demonstration of God's power and a manifestation of His promises. "Therefore prophesy and say to them, 'Thus says the Lord GOD: 'Behold, O My people, I will open your graves and cause you to come up from your graves, and bring you into the land of Israel. Then you shall know that I am the LORD, when I have opened your graves, O My people, and brought you up from your graves. I will put My Spirit in you, and you shall live, and I will place you in your own land. Then you shall know that I, the LORD, have spoken it and performed it,' says the LORD'" (Ezek. 37:12-14).

> When God performs, He fulfills, finishes, gathers, governs, and grants to us that which we need to complete our assignments victoriously.

Notice that the phrase, "I will place you in your own land" was the prophetic fulfillment released in Ezekiel 36. The word of the Lord had come full circle! What if Ezekiel had stopped pressing forward after the bones came together, but there was no breath? That's what we tend to do in the body of Christ. We think we've heard God, we prophesy, but when things don't turn out as we thought, we too often give up, and end up falling short of reaching our prophetic destiny. We do not see the word that God has spoken to us coming to fulfillment. As Ezekiel prophesied through to the end, resurrection power was released so that the graves could be opened and the people set in their own land.

I love this phrase, "Then you will know that I, the Lord, have spoken it and performed it, says the Lord" (v 14). It's one thing for there to be a promise in your life that you know is from God, but it's another thing for that promise to be performed in your life. As we explained in Chapter Two, four levels of agreement and prophesying were necessary for Ezekiel to see the fulfillment of God's word. We cannot be a people that faint easily. Discouragement has no place in us as God's people. If we choose not to back up or stop, but to keep moving forward through the levels of prophecy, God will perform His will in us and bring about prophetic fulfillment!

In Jeremiah 1, we see that God called and commissioned Jeremiah to go forth to bring restoration through change and warning. Verses 11 and 12 summarize what I feel the Lord is saying as we enter the next season ahead: "Moreover, the word of the LORD came to me, saying, 'Jeremiah, what do you see?' And I said, 'I see a branch of an almond tree.' Then the LORD said to me, 'You have seen well, for I am ready to perform My word.'" Perhaps these verses will enable you to pray and trust the Lord to enter into the fullness of His plans concerning your life.

He Causes Eyes to Open!

The phrase, "What do you see?" is all through the Bible in places where Lord would ask this question of His people. When Jesus Christ was born of Mary and the Glory of the Lord manifested in the earth, the shepherds out in the fields, keeping watch over their flocks by night, were startled and even fearful of this manifestation. The angel of the Lord came to them and said not to be afraid for great joy had entered the earth realm. He actually said, "Rejoice, for the unlocking redemptive force for your life has now come to the earth" (paraphrased).

Suddenly, all the heavenly hosts began to praise. Once this host had departed, the shepherds talked among themselves and said, "Let us now go to Bethlehem and *see* this thing that has come to pass which the Lord has made known to us." And when they had seen Him, they told everyone what the angels had said to them.

There will be times of manifestation of His glory in days ahead. Do not fear this manifestation. Be willing to open your eyes to what the angelic hosts are doing around you. See your provision manifest! See your joy restored! See change come into your sphere of authority! Once you *see*, be willing to declare what the Lord is doing!

He is the Branch

"I see a branch of an almond tree." Jeremiah replied to the Lord, when he was asked what he saw. The branch was a symbol of kingship and prosperity (see Dan. 11:7, Job 8:16). The Lord is described as *the* Branch, both righteous and beautiful (see Is. 4:2, Jer. 23:5, Zech 3:8, 6:12). *The* Branch produces branches, and we are branches of the true Vine (see John 15:5,6).

Branches of trees (palm, myrtle, willow, and others) were used ceremonially at the Feast of Tabernacles for making booths (see Neh. 8:15). This symbolically shows us that eventually we, as His branches, will overlay each other to form a covering of safety as we participate in His glory in the earth. Those who understand the Branch will rule.

Back to Jeremiah's response to the Lord, he specifically saw an almond tree. The almond was significant in that it was the first tree to bloom. It was also used as a breeding device to increase Jacob's herds. It was one of the best fruits of the land that was given as a gift. Aaron's rod produced ripe almonds signifying the priesthood to come. The early appearing white bloom of the almond is linked to the graying head which signifies wisdom.

Jeremiah was called to watch and when he saw the almond, it meant that spring was coming. The almond symbolizes "wakeful hastening." As the Lord speaks to us, we need to wake up and watch for things to intensify in our lives. Watch for a new blossoming! Do not fear pruning throughout, for the Branch has come for you to "branch out" and be fruitful. Declare this over your life.

He Comes to Affirm His Glory

The promises of God are "yea and amen." Once we see what God would have us see, He begins to put a "yes" down deep within us. The affirmation of God is also linked with favor. The favor of God upon us causes us to experience pleasure, desire, and delight. He delights in us when we see His path for us and move accordingly.

Favor is also linked with a manifestation of God's glory. Glory, or the the *chabod* of God, is His weightiness. We experience God's glory when we see His honor, splendor, power, wealth, authority, magnificence, dignity, rich, fame, and excellency. Knowing His will and experiencing His glory breaks us out of naïveté, instability, vanity, and the thought processes assuming everything is temporary. Once we experience this affirmation of God's will and glory, we hear God saying to us, "For with God, nothing will be impossible." The affirmation of God causes His Glory to be seen.

He Was and Is Our "I AM"

"I AM" was God's response to Moses' request in Exodus 3:13, 14. This means, "I AM who I AM," "I will be who I will be," or even "I cause to be that which is." God's response is not a "name" that limits God in any way. Rather, it is an affirmation that God is always free to be and act as He wills.

Jesus' "I AM" responses in several New Testament passages suggest more than the simple identifying "I am He." The "I AM" of Mark 6:50 means "I AM Jesus and not a ghost," but suggests the divine "I AM" who alone "tramples down the waves of the sea" (see Job 9:8; Mark 6:48-49) and made the waves hush (see Ps. 107:28-29; compare Mark 4:39). John 8:24 helps us see that Jesus, as the "I AM," is a matter of eternal life and death for us: "You will die in your sins unless you believe that I AM."

Many of us never recognize what His true identity of "I AM" means to us! He is:

* "I AM" is **JEHOVAH** (*Jeh hoh' vuh*). Declare Him as LORD.

* "I AM" is **JEHOVAH-JIREH** (*Jeh hoh' vuh-ji rehh*). Declare that "Yahweh will provide" (Gen. 22:14). It is the name Abraham gave to the place where the Lord provided a sacrifice in place of Isaac. He made Abraham "see" his provision.

* "I AM" is **JEHOVAH- RAPHA** (*Jeh hoh' vuh-ray' fuh*). Declare that "He has healed." In Exodus 15, He is the one who healed them so they could move forward toward the promise. He really was saying, "You need a healer. I AM He who heals."

* "I AM" is **JEHOVAH-NISSI** (*Jeh hoh' vuh-nihs' si*). Declare "Yahweh is my banner." Moses declared Jehovah as Banner and built an altar to Him after defeating the Amalekites (Ex. 17:15). This name is linked with deliverance and miracles.

* "I AM" is **JEHOVAH-SHALOM** (*Jeh hoh' vuh-shah luhm*). Declare "Yahweh is Peace." Gideon built an altar to the God of Peace (Judg. 6:24). "I AM" is the One who

can make you whole. Once Gideon understood this part of His character, he was released to go to war against his enemies. "I AM" has the strategy to defeat your enemies.

♦ "I AM" is **JEHOVAH-SHAMMA** (*Jeh hoh' vuh-shuhm' maw*). Declare Him as "The Lord is There." The Jerusalem of Ezekiel's vision was known by this name. Compare Isaiah 60:19-20; Rev. 21:3. May you sense, feel, and know His presence.

♦ "I AM" is **JEHOVAH-TSIDKENU** (*Jeh hoh' vuh-tsihd kee' new*). Declare Him as "The Lord [is] our righteousness" (Jer. 23:6; 33:16). The name is applied to a future Davidic king who would lead his people to do what is right and thus bring peace (23:6) and restore the city of Jerusalem (33:16). You are the righteousness of God in Christ Jesus!

Know I AM as the Prince of Peace

Peace is a state of rest, quietness, and calmness. Peace is an absence of strife leading to tranquility. Peace denotes wholeness – body, soul, and spirit – and perfect well-being. Peace includes harmonious relationships between God and humans, between one another, and between nations and families. Jesus, as Prince of Peace, gives peace to those who call upon Him for personal salvation.

Luke 1:79 says He came "to give light to those who sit in darkness and the shadow of death, to guide our feet into the way of peace. So the child grew and became strong in spirit." I believe this is the will of the Prince of Peace in our lives. Matthew 10:34 says, "Do not think I came to bring peace on earth. I did not come to bring peace but a sword." These two statements seem contrary.

However, what the Lord is saying is "Let me cut away every earthly tie that distracts you from *My* best will in heaven for your life. I long to see you whole and filled with peace. So let Me cut away that which will keep you from being whole and experiencing My covenant blessings."

God is Ready to Perform His Word!

When God is ready to move, it means He is watching, waking, hastening, and anticipating the perfect time to align with His saints in the earth and release His will to be manifested in our midst. To be ready means that He is sleepless, alert, vigilant, and on the look-out to cause the supernatural door in heaven to open and pour out His will in the earth. To be ready means He is watchfully looking for the opportunity to care for us in a new way. To be ready means He is watching to begin to build and plant in the earth that which He has blueprinted in heaven.

When God was ready to move to give His Son to us as a gift, He began to order and orchestrate events for that release. He does the same thing in your life. Watch for the ordered events. Have an assurance He is watching over you. Watch with Him so that when He opens doors for you, you go through into a new dimension of freedom, victory and glory.

Once we are abiding in Him, He can accomplish, confirm, and continue His will in our lives to bring us into His full plan. He can cause us to endure our circumstances and enemies so that they do not stop us from advancing into the ultimate victory He has for our lives.

To perform means to stir up, strengthen, succeed, accomplish, advance, and appoint. To perform means He will release industrious ability within us, so that as we journey on the path He has given us and sacrifice before Him, we will feel His presence and power. To perform also means to assemble, fight, muster together, and wait upon the war ahead. In waiting He comes to our aid to demonstrate His love and ability in our lives. When He performs He fulfills, finishes, gathers, governs, and grants to us that which we need to complete our assignments victoriously. "Blessed is she (or we) that believe. For there shall be a performance of those things that were told to her (or us) from the Lord" (Luke 1:45, parentheses added).

He was sent "to perform the mercy promised to our fathers and to remember His holy covenant" (Luke 1:72). "And being fully persuaded that, what He had promised, He was able also to perform" (Rom. 4:21). There will be a performance! "Be confident of this very thing, that He who has begun a good work in you will perform it to the day of Jesus Christ" (Phil. 1:6). Let Him be the performance of your life. Lay down your own performance and enter into His!

We hope this book has helped you as you recognize when God is speaking and helped you to embrace the voice of God in your life. May our Lord richly bless you as you seek to hear His voice and obey His will for your life! We are praying for you to hear the voice of God in a new way.

Appendix One:
Dream Symbol Interpretation

As you will notice, many of the following symbols may have conflicting interpretations assigned to them, some positive and some negative. This list is only meant to be a general guide. The symbol always needs to be interpreted in light of the context of the dream or vision, and in light of what the symbol means to the dreamer, and by the guidance of the Holy Spirit.

Numbers

ONE. Unity, God, beginning, first, rank, order, new.

TWO. Division, Judge, separate, discern, agreement, witness; union (two becoming one).

THREE. The Trinity, Deity, conform, obey, copy, imitate, likeness, tradition, completeness, perfect, testimony; connected with the bodily resurrection of Christ and His people.

FOUR. The earth (four winds, four corners), reign, rule, kingdom, creation; unsaved or fleshy man.

FIVE. Grace, redemption, atonement, life, the Cross, government (five-fold gifts), works, service, bondage (including debt, sickness, phobias, etc.), taxes, prison, sin, motion.

SIX. Humanity, The Beast, Satan, flesh, carnal, idol; manifestation of sin.

SEVEN. Complete, all, finished, rest, perfection.

EIGHT. Put off (as in putting off "the old self"), sanctification, manifest, reveal, new beginnings, resurrection, die, death; new order of things.

NINE. Manifestation of the Holy Spirit, harvest, fruitfulness, fruition, fruit of the womb, finality, fullness; perfection or divine completeness.

TEN. Judgment, try or trial, test, temptation, law, order, government, restoration, responsibility, tithe, Antichrist kingdom; testimony.

ELEVEN. Mercy, end, finish, last stop, incompleteness, disorganization, disintegration, lawlessness, disorder, the Antichrist; judgment.

TWELVE. Joined, united, govern, government, oversight, apostolic fullness, the Holy City of God; governmental perfection.

THIRTEEN. Rebellion, backsliding, apostasy, revolution, rejection, double blessing, double cursing; depravity.

FOURTEEN. Passover, double, recreate, reproduce, disciple, servant, bond slave or employee; deliverance or salvation.

FIFTEEN. Free, grace, liberty, sin covered, honor; rest.

SIXTEEN. Free spirited, without boundaries, without law, without sin, salvation; love.

SEVENTEEN. Spiritual order, incomplete, immature, undeveloped, childish; victory.

EIGHTEEN. Put on (as in the Spirit of Christ), judgment, destruction, captivity, overcome; bondage.

NINETEEN. Barren, ashamed, repentant, selflessness, without self-righteousness; faith.

TWENTY. Holy, tried and approved, tried and found wanting; redemption.

TWENTY-ONE. Exceeding sinfulness, of sin.

TWENTY-TWO. Light.

TWENTY-THREE. Death.

TWENTY-FOUR. Priestly courses, governmental perfection.

TWENTY-FIVE. The forgiveness of sins.

TWENTY-SIX. The Gospel of Christ.

TWENTY-SEVEN. Preaching of the Gospel.

TWENTY-EIGHT. Eternal life.

TWENTY-NINE. Departure.

THIRTY. Consecration, maturity for ministry.

THIRTY-TWO. Covenant.

THIRTY-THREE. Promise.

THIRTY-FOUR. Naming of a son.

THIRTY-FIVE. Hope.

THIRTY-SIX. Enemy.

THIRTY-SEVEN. The Word of God.

THIRTY-EIGHT. Slavery.

THIRTY-NINE. Disease.

FORTY. Probation, testing, ending in victory or defeat; trials.

FORTY-TWO. Israel's oppression, the Lord's advent to the earth.

FORTY-FIVE. Preservation.

FIFTY. Pentecost, liberty, freedom, jubilee; Holy Spirit.

SIXTY. Pride.

SIXTY-SIX. Idol worship.

SEVENTY. Prior to increase, multitude; universality, Israel and her restoration.

SEVENTY-FIVE. Separation, cleansing, purification.

HUNDRED. Fullness, full measure, full recompense, full reward, etc.; God's election of grace, children of promise.

ONE HUNDRED NINETEEN. The resurrection day; Lord's day.

ONE HUNDRED TWENTY. End of all flesh, beginning of life in the Spirit; divine period of probation.

ONE HUNDRED FORTY-FOUR. God's ultimate creation and redemption; the Spirit-guided life.

ONE HUNDRED FIFTY-THREE. God's elect, revival, ingathering, harvest; fruit bearing.

TWO HUNDRED. Insufficiency.

SIX HUNDRED. Warfare.

SIX-SIX-SIX. Antichrist, Satan, mark of the damned, mark of the man who is a beast; the number of the beast.

EIGHT-EIGHT-EIGHT. The first resurrection saints.

THOUSAND. Maturity, full stature, mature service, mature judgment, etc.; divine completeness and the glory of God.

Colors

AMBER. The glory of God.

BLACK. Lack, sin, ignorance, grief, mourning, gloomy, evil, ominous, famine, burned, death.

BLUE. Spiritual, divine revelation, visitation, authority, Holy Spirit, depressed (as in "feeling blue"), male infant, hope. (Medium or dark blue can be God's Spirit or Word, blessing, healing, good will. Very light blue can be spirit of man, evil spirit, corrupt).

BROWN. Dead (as in plant life), repentant, born again, without spirit.

CRIMSON. Blood atonement, sacrifice, death.

GRAY. Unclear, vague, not specific, hazy, deception, hidden, crafty, false doctrine (gray hair can be wisdom, age, or weakness).

GREEN. Life, mortal, flesh, carnal, envy, inexperienced, immature renewal (evergreen can be eternal life or immortal).

ORANGE. Danger, great jeopardy, harm (a common color combination is orange and black together which usually signifies great evil or danger; bright or fire orange can be power, force, energy).

PINK. Flesh, sensual, immoral, moral (as in "a heart of flesh"); chaste, a female infant.

PURPLE. Royal, kingship, rule (good or evil), majestic, noble.

RED. Passion, emotion, anger, hatred, lust, sin, enthusiasm, zeal, war, bloodshed, death.

WHITE. Pure, without mixture, light, righteousness, holiness of God, Christ, the angels or saints, blameless, innocence.

YELLOW. Gift, marriage, family, honor, deceitful gift, timidity, fear, cowardliness.

Creatures

ALLIGATOR. Ancient, evil out of the past (through inherited or personal sin), danger, destruction, evil spirit.

ANT. Industrious, wise, diligent prepared for the future, nuisance, stinging or angry words.

ASS (DONKEY). Lowliness, patience, strength, endurance, service.

ASS (WILD MULE). Untamed human nature, stubborn, self-willed, unsubdued, depraved, obnoxious, unbelief.

BAT. Witchcraft, unstable, flighty, fear.

BEAR. Destroyer, evil curse (through inheritance or personal sin, including financial loss or hardship), economic loss, danger, opposition, evil cunning, cruel, strong, ferocious.

BEAVER. Industrious, busy, diligent, clever, ingenious.

BEES. Produce sweetness, power to sting, host of people, affliction, busybody, gossip.

BIRD. Spirit, Holy Spirit, demon, man, gossip, message (see CROW/RAVEN, DOVE, EAGLE, OWL, VULTURE).

BULL. Persecution, spiritual warfare, opposition, accusation, slander, threat, economic increase.

BUTTERFLY. Freedom, flighty, fragile, temporary glory.

CALF. Increase, prosperity, idolatry, false worship, stubbornness, prayers, praise, thanksgiving, skipping.

CAMEL. Burden-bearer, servant, endurance, long journey, not graceful.

CAT. Self-willed, not trainable, predator, unclean spirit, bewitching charm, stealthy, sneaky, crafty, deception, self-pity, something precious in the context of a personal pet.

CHICKEN. Fear, cowardliness (hen can be protection, gossip, motherhood; rooster can be boasting, bragging, proud; chick can be defenseless, innocent).

CROW/RAVEN. Confusion, outspoken, operating in envy or strife, hateful, direct path, unclean, God's minister of justice or provision.

DEER. Graceful, swift, sure-footed, agile, timid.

DOG. Strife, contention, offense, unclean spirit, unbelievers (pet dog can be something precious, friend, loyal; dog wagging tail can be friend, acceptance; dog biting can be rewarding evil for good, betrayal, unthankful; barking dog can be warning, incessant nuisance, annoyance; dog trailing game can be persistent, obsession; rabid dog can be single-minded pursuit of evil, contagious evil, persecution, great danger; bulldog can be unyielding, stubborn; watchdog can be watchman, elder, minister [good or bad], alert, beware).

DOVE. Holy Spirit, gentleness, sacrifice.

DRAGON. Satan, evil spirits, Antichrist forces.

EAGLE. Leader, prophet (true or false), see from above, minister, fierce predator, sorcerer, strength, swift.

ELEPHANT. Invincible or thick-skinned, not easily offended, powerful, large.

FISH. Souls of humanity (both clean and unclean), character or motive.

FOX. Subtlety, deception, cunning, false prophet, wicked leader, hidden sin, sly and evil people.

FROG. Demon, witchcraft, curse, evil words, puffed up, unclean.

GOAT. Sinner, unbelief, stubborn, argumentative, negative person, blamed for other's wrongdoing.

HAWK. Predator, sorcerer, evil spirit, warrior, unclean.

HORSE. Strength, swiftness, power, spiritual support, power of the flesh, spiritual warfare, age.

LION. Dominion, Christ, king, regal, bold, power, Satan, religious tradition, courage, royalty.

MICE. Devourer, curse, plague, timid.

MONKEY. Foolishness, clinging, mischief, dishonesty, addiction.

MOTH. Deterioration, destructive, deceitful, undetected trouble, corruption.

OWL. Circumspect, wisdom, demon, curse, night bird.

PIG. Ignorance, hypocrisy, religious unbelievers, unclean people, selfish, gluttonous, vicious, vengeful.

RABBIT. Increase, fast growth, multiplication (hare can be Satan and his evil spirits).

RACCOON. Mischief, night raider, rascal, thief, bandit, deceitful.

RAT. Unclean, wicked person, jerk, devourer, plague, betrayer.

ROACH. Infestation, unclean spirits, hidden sin.

SCORPION. Sin nature, lust of the flesh, temptation, deception, accusation, destruction, danger, a whip.

SERPENT (SNAKE). Curse, demon, deception, threat, danger, hatred, slander, witchcraft, wisdom.

SHEEP. Chant, the people of God, innocent.

SPIDER. Evil, sin, deception, false doctrine, temptation, (web can be snares, lies).

TIGER. Danger, powerful minister (both good and evil).

VULTURE. Scavenger, unclean, impure, evil person or spirit, all seeing, waiting for evil opportunity.

WOLF. Predator, devourer, false prophet, person seeking own gain, wicked and false teachers, destroyer of God's flock.

Other

ACID. Bitter, offense, carrying a grudge, hatred, sarcasm.

APPLES. Fruit, words, sin, temptation, appreciation, fruit of the Spirit.

ARM. Strength or weakness, savior, deliverer, helper, aid, reaching out, striker.

ASHES. Memories, repentance, ruin, destruction.

AUTOMOBILE. Life, person, ministry.

AUTUMN. End, completion, change, repentance.

BABY. New beginning, new idea, dependant, helpless, innocent, sin.

BED. Rest, salvation, meditation, intimacy, peace, covenant (marriage, natural, or evil), self-made.

BICYCLE. Works, works of the flesh, legalism, self-righteousness, working out life's difficulties, messenger.

BLOOD. Life of the flesh, covenant, murder, defiled, unclean, pollution, purging, testimony, witness, guilt.

BOAT. Support, life, person, recreation, spare time, personal ministry.

BRASS. Word of God or man, judgment, hypocrisy, self-justification, fake, human tradition.

BROTHER-IN-LAW. Partiality or adversary, fellow minister, problem relationship, partner, oneself, natural brother-in-law.

CLOUDS. Change or covering, trouble, distress, threatening, thoughts of trouble, confusion, hidden.

DANCING. Worship, idolatry, prophesying, joy, romance, seduction, lewdness.

DIAMOND. Hard, hardheaded, hardhearted, unchangeable, eternal, gift of the Spirit, something valuable or precious.

DOOR. Entrance, Christ, opportunity, way, avenue, mouth.

DREAMING (WHEN DREAMING). A message within a message, aspiration, vision.

DROWNING. Overcome, self-pity, depression, grief, sorrow, temptation, excessive debt.

DRUGS. Influence, spell, sorcery, witchcraft, control, legalism, medicine, healing.

EARTHQUAKE. Upheaval, change by crisis, repentance, trial, God's judgment, disaster, trauma, shock.

EATING. Partake, participate, experience, out-working, covenant, agreement, friendship, fellowship, devour, consume.

ELEVATOR. Changing position, going into the spirit realm, elevated or demoted.

EYES. Desire, covetousness, passion, lust, revelation, understanding.

FALLING. Unsupported, loss of support (financial, moral, public, etc.), trial, succumb, backsliding.

FATHER. Authority, God, author, originator, source, inheritance, tradition, custom, Satan, natural father.

FATHER-IN-LAW. Law, authoritative relationship based on law, legalism, problem authoritative relationship, natural father-in-law.

FEET. Heart, walk, way, thoughts (meditation), offense, stubborn (unmovable), rebellion (kicking), sin.

FINGER. Feeling, sensitivity, discernment, conviction, works, accusation (as in pointing finger), instruction.

FLOWERS. Glory, temporary, gifts, romance.

FOREIGNER. Alien, not of God, of the flesh, demonic.

FOREST. Foreboding, fearful place, often associated with confusion or without direction.

FRIEND. Self; the character or circumstance of one's friend reveals something about oneself; sometimes one friend represents another (look for another with the same name, initials, hair color, etc.); or could represent actual friend.

GOLD. Glory or wisdom, truth, something precious, righteousness, glory of God, self-glorification.

GRANDCHILD. Heir, oneself, inherited blessing or iniquity, one's spiritual legacy, actual grandchild.

GRANDPARENT. Past, spiritual inheritance (good or evil), actual grandparent.

GRAPES. Fruit, spirit of promise, fruit of the Spirit, promise of wrath.

HAIR. Covering, covenant, humanity, doctrine, tradition, old sinful nature.

HANDS. Works, deeds (good or evil), labor, service, idolatry, spiritual warfare.

IRON. Strength, powerful, invincible, stronghold, stubborn.

KISS. Agreement, covenant, enticement, betrayal, covenant breaker, deception, seduction, friend.

KNEES. Submission, obey, worship, service, stubborn, unyielding.

LEAD. Weight, wickedness, sin, burden, judgment, fool or foolishness.

MECHANIC. Minister, Christ, prophet, pastor, counselor.

MIRROR. God's Word or one's heart, looking at oneself, looking back, memory, past, vanity.

MISCARRIAGE. Abort, failure, loss, repentance, unjust judgment.

MONEY. Power, provision, wealth, natural talents and skills, spiritual riches, power, authority, trust in human strength, covetousness.

MOTHER. Source, Church, love, kindness, spiritual or natural mother.

MOTHER-IN-LAW. Legalism, meddler, trouble, natural mother-in-law.

NUDITY. Uncovered or flesh, self-justification, self-righteousness, impure, ashamed, stubborn, temptation, lust, sexual control, exhibitionism, truth, honest, nature.

OIL. Anointing, (clear oil can be the Holy Spirit anointing, healing; dirty oil can be unclean spirits, hate, lust, seduction, deception, slick, danger of slipping).

PEN/PENCIL. Tongue, indelible words, covenant, agreement, contract, vow, publish, record, permanent, unforgettable, gossip.

PREGNANCY. In process, sin or righteousness in process, desire, anticipation, expectancy.

PUMPKIN. Witchcraft, deception, snare, witch, trick.

RAIN. Life, revival, Holy Spirit, Word of God, depression, trial, disappointment.

SILVER. Knowledge of God (redemption), knowledge of the world (idolatry).

SISTER. Spiritual sister, Church, self, natural sister.

SPRING. New beginning, revival, fresh start, renewal, regeneration, salvation, refreshing.

STONE. Witness, word, testimony, person, precept, accusations, persecution.

STORM. Disturbance, change, spiritual warfare, judgment, sudden calamity or destruction, trial, persecution, opposition, witchcraft.

SUMMER. Harvest, opportunity, trial, heat of affliction.

TABLE. Communion, agreement, covenant, conference, provision (under the table can be deceitful dealings, hidden motives, evil intent).

TIN. Dross, waste, worthless, cheap, purification.

TRAIN. Continuous, unceasing work, connected, fast, the Church.

TREE. Person or covering, leader, shelter, false worship, evil influence (oak can be strong shelter, willow can be sorrow, evergreen can be eternal life).

TUNNEL. Passage, transition, way of escape, troubling experience, trial, hope.

VAN. Family (natural or Church), family ministry, fellowship.

WATER. Spirit, Word, the spirit of man or the spirit of the enemy, unstable.

WIND. Spirit or doctrine, Holy Spirit, demonic or strong opposition, idle words.

WINDOW. Revealed, truth, prophecy, revelation, understanding, avenue of blessing, exposed, an unguarded opening for a thief to enter.

WINE (or Strong Drink). Intoxicant, strong emotion (such as joy, anger, hate, or sorrow), Spirit of God or spirit of man, revelation, truth, witchcraft, delusion, mocker.

WINTER. Barren, death, dormant, waiting, cold, unfriendly.

WOOD. Life, temporary, flesh, humanity, carnal reasoning, lust, eternal, spiritual building material.

WRESTLING. Striving, deliverance, resistance, persistence, trial, tribulation, spirit attempting to gain control.

This list of dream symbol interpretations has been compiled from the following references:

Kevin J. Conner, *Interpreting the Symbols and Types* (Bible Temple Publishing).

Jane Hamon, *Dreams and Visions* (Regal Books).

Ira Milligan, *Understanding the Dreams You Dream* (Treasure House).

Ed F. Vallowe, *Keys to Scripture Numerics* (Ed F. Vallowe Evangelistic Association).

For further explanation or biblical references on any of the listed symbols, or for more complete lists, please see these references.

Appendix Two:

Recommended Reading

Bickle, Mike. *Growing in the Prophetic.* Orlando, FL: Creation House, 1996.

Connor, Kevin J. *Interpreting the Symbols and Types.* Portland, OR: Bible Temple Publishing, 1992.

Cooke, Graham. *Developing Your Prophetic Gifting.* Kent, England: Sovereign World, 1994.

Deere, Jack. *Surprised by the Voice of God.* Grand Rapids, MI: Zondervan Publishing House, 1996.

Hamon, Bill. *Prophets and Personal Prophecy.* Shippensburg, PA: Destiny Image, 1987.

Hamon, Jane. *Dreams and Visions.* Ventura, CA: Regal Books, 2000.

Jacobs, Cindy. *The Voice of God.* Ventura, CA: Regal Books, 1995.

Joyner, Rick. *The Prophetic Ministry.* Charlotte, NC: Morningstar Publications, 1997.

Lord, Peter. *Hearing God.* Grand Rapids, MI: Baker Books, 1988.

Milligan, Ira. *Every Dreamer's Handbook.* Shippensburg, PA: Treasure House, 2000.

_____. *Understanding the Dreams You Dream.* Shippensburg, PA: Treasure House, 1997.

Vallowe, Ed. F. *Biblical Mathematics.* Columbia, SC: The
Olive Press, 1998.

Yocum, Bruce. *Prophecy.* Ann Arbor, MI: Servant
Publications, 1976.

Recommended Tape Series:

School of the Prophets. Eight-tape set and manual featuring
Chuck Pierce, Robert Heidler, Barbara Wentroble and
Jim Hodges. Available through Glory of Zion
Ministries, P.O. Box 1601, Denton, TX, 76201; phone
940-382-1166.

Subject Index

If you enjoyed this book, be sure to read the companion book...

The Best is Yet Ahead
Chuck D. Pierce
& Rebecca Wagner Sytsema

God has a wonderful destiny for every life, but many Christians will die never having accomplished all that God has for them. This book gives dynamic, life-giving answers to help believers reach their potential as they wrestle with questions including:

- How can I break out of desolation?

- What seven principles do I need to know to press toward my destiny?

- How do I "war" with a prophetic word from God?

- How do I deal with hope deferred?

This book is full of rich, fresh insight for finding God's direction in your life, your family, and your territory. As you read you will understand how to press toward prophetic fulfillment and gain new hope that the best is yet ahead!

Christian Living
Paperback • 111p
ISBN 1-58502-023-0

Ridding Your Home of Spiritual Darkness

Chuck D. Pierce
& Rebecca Wagner Sytsema

Christians are often completely unaware of how the enemy has gained access to their homes through what they own. This practical, easy-to-read book can be used by any Christian to pray through their home and property in order to close the door to the enemy and experience richer spiritual life. Included are chapters on:

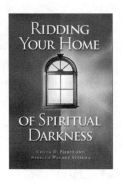

- Understanding spiritual darkness

- Children

- Generational curses

- Spiritual discernment

- Land and property

- A ten-step guide to praying through your home

Christian Living
Paperback • 80p
ISBN 1-58502-008-7

WAGNER
LEADERSHIP INSTITUTE

Founded by Dr. C. Peter Wagner, Wagner Leadership Institute (WLI) trains and equips men and women for leadership in local churches and other ministries.

This radical new approach to education emphasizes practical ministry experience, anointing, and impartation. Because practical training and impartation are the goals of each course, no grades are given for courses, events, or training experiences taken for credit. Nor are there exams. Rather, field research, apprenticeship, mentoring, and ministry experience are deemed as valuable as library research or classroom attendance. Our goal is to equip leaders with the necessary skills for effective ministry. Entrance requirements are not based on academics, but on age, ministry experience, and maturity.

WLI provides an earned training credential for church and ministry leaders who desire ordination, licensing, or other forms of public recognition by awarding diplomas for Associate of Practical Ministry, Bachelor of Practical Ministry, Master of Practical Ministry, and Doctor of Practical Ministry.

For more information on Wagner Leadership Institute visit our website at:

www.wagnerleadership.org

or call us at:

1-800-683-9630